SHADOWS
OF THE
PAST

SHADOWS
OF THE
PAST

*The Story of WW2 Wellington Bomber Pilot
W/O 'Tubby' Gaunt RAFVR*

Paul Phillip Gaunt

Fort Royal

Dedication

For my loving wife, Denise, without whom this book would probably not have been written.

SHADOWS OF THE PAST
The Story of WW2 Bomber Pilot W/O Tubby Gaunt RAFVR.

© Paul Phillip Gaunt, 2008.
ISBN: 978-0-9557517-1-4

All rights reserved. No part of this publication may be reproduced, stored in a retrieval system or transmitted in any form or by any means without prior permission from the author and publisher.

First published 2008 by Fort Royal.

Fort Royal
Tel: 07921 503105

www.FortRoyal.co.uk

Design by Fort Royal, printed & bound in the UK.

Distributed by JAM Secretarial Services, 31 Schofield Road, Oakham, Rutland, Leics LE15 6FW, Tel: 01572 770346.

Contents

Foreword: p. 6
Introduction: p. 7

Chapter One: p. 16
Chapter Two: p. 24
Chapter Three: p. 29
Chapter Four: p. 40
Chapter Five: p. 99
Chapter Six: p. 114
Chapter Seven: p. 166
Chapter Eight: p. 182

Postscript: p. 208

Acknowledgements: p. 211
Bibliography: p. 213

Appendix: p. 214

Foreword

Books on military history usually deal with a specific operation or campaign, or they describe the wartime contribution of someone who has become well known because of it. This book is quite different. Although the aim is to describe the wartime experiences of one man, the book gives the reader, in graphic detail, a very clear picture of what life was like for the thousands of ordinary unsung heroes who, in spite of the odds against survival, flew day after day on bombing missions in Europe throughout World War Two.

Being a near neighbour, I knew of Paul Gaunt's painstaking research over 15 years into the wartime experiences of his father, and I am very pleased to see that the results of his research can now be shared by others. His research was not just confined to pouring over extensive records, but widened to finding and talking to many of his father's wartime colleagues and gathering together his father's Wellington crew. Paul also made several visits to Croatia, to see where his father's last mission ended and to talk to those who remember the circumstances at the time.

Like some who survived when many of their friends had not, Tubby Gaunt never talked of his wartime experiences and his son's quest to find out about them was sparked entirely by a chance visit to a museum. One can understand his surprise and delight when the more he looked into his father's wartime experiences, the more he found. Tubby Gaunt had certainly done his bit. He had flown extensively from UK as a gunner on bombing and anti shipping missions and later as a pilot from Italy on raids against German forces and to supply the Jugoslav partisans. He had survived not just the usual aircrew trials of enemy action, technical failures and adverse weather, but also a mid air collision in England and in Croatia a crash landing in an area and in weather where the chances of surviving the crash and then being rescued by friends were very slim.

The reader is treated to a comprehensive account as the author also provides the wider background to this World War Two story and is therefore better able to put it into context.

<u>Air Marshal Sir John Sutton KCB, KStJ</u>

Introduction

It has been some 15 years since, by chance, I stumbled across information that has changed my life and set me on a search for information about my father, Philip Gaunt, who reached the rank of Pilot Warrant Officer during his six years service in the Royal Air Force Voluntary Reserve (RAFVR) throughout the Second World War of 1939-45. Uncovering a unique career, through my persistent diligence and at times gut feelings, I have found the 'other man' in my father, that until 1992 I was completely unaware of. His story has given me admiration for a man who was more than just a father to my brother Terry, sisters Ann and Christina, and I. Through my investigations, I have been able to follow my father's footsteps using his detailed logbooks, service career records and later, whilst in Yugoslavia, his bomb aimer's diary of events after icing up and crash landing in Croatia, as it is now.

A fresh faced 'Tubby', September 1939, at Manston, Kent, during basic training.

Philip Gaunt's pre-war training was with the Civil Air Guard 1938-39 and was entirely voluntary. He was extremely keen to fly and, like many other people, foresaw the approaching war. So Philip, on August 4th, 1939, enlisted in the RAFVR for a period of five years; he was 22 years of age. After kitting out at RAF Receiving Station Cardington and basic training at Manston, Tubby was selected for wireless operator/air gunnery training. This was a disappointment, however, as he had initially been recommended for pilot training. Nonetheless Philip was not despondent and put all into his training. This took him to Cranwell for signals training, and No 1 Wing, No 4 Bombing &

Shadows of the Past

Gunnery School Fiskerton. On January 18th, 1941, Philip moved to No 14 Operational Training Unit (OTU) at Cottesmore, Rutland, and then to 49 Squadron at Scampton, near Lincoln, on September 9th, 1941; there started his first tour as Wireless Operator/Air Gunner on Handley-Page Hampden Bombers.

Philip's first tour of 1941-42 was very varied, with 'gardening' operations (dropping mines in the sea) around Heligoland (in the main German sea lanes), bombing ships at Brest harbour, France, the pocket-battleships *Scharnhorst* and *Prince Eugen*, and bombing of not only Berlin, the Reich capital, but also the industrial cities of Essen-Cologne, and Dortmund, all in the Ruhr valley.

My father was to have a nickname, which, because of his portly nature, was 'Tubby'. So Tubby Gaunt it was and is the reference name I found when reading about him, after buying a book called 'Wellington the Geodetic Giant' (by Martin Bowman). Through the author, I contacted Maurice Sandell, who was the bomb aimer in Tubby's Wellington crew in Foggia, Southern Italy. Maurice had recalled his Yugoslavian experience in the book. On contacting the author and finding Maurice, it kick-started, for me, a most interesting and exciting experience. After gathering information on a part-time basis only, because of work and family commitments, for 15 years, I have now reached a point where I must collate all this information into some order and produce this story. I can only assume from Tubby's progression from W/O A/G to Pilot, that he achieved his ambition to become a pilot and skipper of his own aircraft.

From Scampton Tubby flew 22 operations, during which time the obsolete Hampden bomber was withdrawn and crews converted first to the ill-fated Avro Manchester, with its unpredictable Vulture engines, then to the famous Avro Lancaster. Tubby then remustered to undergo pilot training. Being accepted and put through initial training at Marshals of Cambridge, he was immediately posted to Witbank and later to Petersberg, South Africa, to undergo his *ab initio* pilot training. This period of over 12 months resulted in Tubby gaining his wings, moving up to Quastina in Palestine (No 77 OTU), picking his crew and training on the Wellington Mk X. His next squadron, with which he served for 4 months, was 37

Shadows of the Past

*From left: Clarice, Maurice,
Philip (Tubby) & Arthur 1926/27.*

*Tubby (far left) next to his sister, Clarice & my grandfather, Percy, at Maurice &
Tilly's wedding, November 14th, 1940. Arthur, Tubby's brother, is behind
the groom with other family members.*

Squadron at Foggia (Tortorella), Italy. Later, because the new American Consolidated Liberator B-24 bomber was replacing the Wellington, new Liberator crews were posted to 37 Squadron; those Wellington crews without Liberator experience were posted to 70 Squadron, also at Tortorella.

At this time it was the elements, however, not so much the enemy, that were responsible for most losses. During these late stages of the war, Tubby and crew's exit from hostilities was caused not by enemy action but by ice: on January 8th, 1945, they crash-landed in the mountains of Gorski Kotar, near the Croatia-Slovenia border, in a small hamlet called Vode, about 5 kilometres from Gerovo. Fortunately Marshal Tito's partisans were on hand to help the crew and pass them through various safe houses, crossing the German lines, down to the coastal town of Zadar on the Adriatic Coast, then on to a British destroyer and back to Bari in Italy. Next, after de-briefing, they went onwards by troopship to Liverpool and home for four weeks survivor's leave. After the crew's harrowing experiences, though, they were never again to meet all together. However, I had the pleasure of finding them all and putting them back in touch, which took some years. Frank (Geordie) Hazelden, the rear gunner, is now living in Australia, a retired lighthouse keeper somewhere on the Barrier Reef; Dave (Jock) Scanlan, the wireless operator, lives in British Columbia and is a retired schoolteacher; Maurice (Scats) Sandell, the bomb aimer, lives on the outskirts of Norwich, a retired civil servant; sadly Jack (Mack) McMellin died 1994, he was a retired company director who later lived in Cumbria. Tubby himself was a tyre salesman and died after an illness in 1976, having lived in or around Leicester all his life.

Reflecting on my father's story, the one thing that has stuck in my mind was the appalling loss of life, aircrew and ground crew alike. The early years' losses at times must have weighed heavily on the young men who carried on the fight against the Nazis. How my father carried on, apparently undaunted by the continuous pressure and losses of his fellow aircrews, I will never know. Surely, an experience he went through would have occasionally come into conversation, but no, I can never remember his wartime exploits ever being discussed; good, or the many, bad memories he kept to himself.

Shadows of the Past

Tubby was one of six children, five boys and Clarice the only girl. Of the boys, Maurice, the eldest, served in the RAF as a plotter on the south coast of England, Philip (Tubby) in Bomber Command, Arthur was an Artificer in the Royal Artillery, mainly unjamming artillery pieces in North Africa and Italy. Peter was a 'Bevin Boy' and worked in Ellistown colliery in Leicestershire and last, but not least, John, who was too young for active service, was at school during the war years. Clarice, who had married before the war, was a telephonist at the fire station in Cleckheaton, Yorkshire, until 1941 when her daughter Carol was born, after which she became a housewife. Tubby's father was a hairdresser and died in 1953, his mother, a housewife, having died at the young age of 49.

The idea of writing a book was conceived in my thoughts many years ago, although the actual story only came to light in the spring of 1992. I was going through a phase of fatigue which was due to workload, generating a desire to 'get away from it all' feeling. Sylvia, my first wife, and I had decided to go away for a weekend, actually it was Saturday afternoon as we drove down the M5 Motorway to Bath, which I had passed through often, but had never looked around, an old Roman town with many ancient artifacts. Our stay was brief, just overnight to be precise. Making our way towards home late on the Sunday morning we decided to take the much prettier route up the old Fosse Way. With lunch in mind, we stopped at the old Gloucestershire village of Morton-in-Marsh. After a very nice pub lunch we enjoyed a walk around this very pleasant village, and found a picture of a Wellington bomber on show in the local building society window. The accompanying card, displayed in the corner of the frame, advertised the Wellington Art & Aviation Museum, across the road about 300 yards away and just around the corner. Always having had an avid interest in the last war, especially the RAF, Sylvia and I walked over to have a look, with my instructions not to be too long because of getting home to organise the coming week's work. We stayed for almost an hour, but I could easily have stayed all day! Remembering that during the war my father had, for a time, flown in Wellingtons, I asked if there was a book or books about this aeroplane. The gentleman there informed me that a book called 'Wellington the Geodetic Giant' would give me an insight into the aircraft and the crews who flew them in combat. Again, being rushed to leave, I hastily purchased the book, hurried to the car, and drove straight home.

Shadows of the Past

The usual Sunday evening then passed, me checking the personnel and destinations thereof for the week's work ahead, telephoning my customer and confirming everything was in order. Later that evening, I had a quick look at the book I had bought that afternoon; settling down with a large whisky and a cigar, I browsed through the photographs. I always look at the photographs first, hoping that perhaps one day I might see a photo of my late father, who I thought may have been a sergeant pilot, remembering the few times he spoke about the war and some of the places he had been to, but my boyhood memories were very vague. The index was searched and, to my astonishment, there was a reference to a 'Tubby Gaunt' on pages 146-7-8-9.

Quickly turning to these pages, I read with avid interest and an urgency I had not experienced before, the story told by a Sergeant Maurice Sandel of the period in Italy 1944-45, about 37 and 70 Squadrons, referring to Tubby Gaunt regularly. I turned to my wife Sylvia and excitedly told her about what I had read. Do you think this could be my father? Sylvia said you must phone your mother and ask her. This I did and on being connected, asked her what, if any, was my father's RAF nickname. "Tubby", she replied, and explained that when my father came home on leave with comrades, and even after the war, she was called 'Mrs. Tubby'. My father was 5 feet 7 inches tall and of a portly nature, so the nickname was appropriate. Most, if not all, of the aircrew members had nicknames, as I was later to find out. The excitement of this find gave me a feeling of great pride and admiration for my father, who I know was only a small part in the enormous organisation and operations of the RAF during the Second World War. I had to find out more to satisfy my appetite for information of the actions fought during those long war years of 1939-45.

I was sure that my brother had our father's flying logbooks and so contacted him. A complete copy of these personal records confirmed that our father's total number of operations was 44. The early years (1941-42) in the bombing offensive against Germany he had spent as an air gunner and wireless operator before training to be a pilot in 1943 and subsequently carrying out operations (1944-45) in Italy.

Shadows of the Past

This story is about a man who was from an ordinary working class family. Before the Second World War, in 1932, his first job was an apprentice motor mechanic at a small garage in the village of Blaby, only a mile from his home on the Winchester Road in Countesthorpe, approximately 5 miles south of Leicester. In 1937, he became a battery salesman in the motor trade. He enjoyed a comfortable lifestyle with his father, brothers and sister and played the violin in a small dance band. He joined the Civil Air Guard in 1938, and about this time met my mother; they were married on May 6th, 1939. He settled down and moved to a small semi-detached house, No 79 Kingston Avenue, Wigston Fields, a suburb of south Leicester.

After volunteering for the RAFVR, father was called up and duly reported for duty on September 2nd, 1939, the day after Hitler invaded Poland and only a day before Britain and France declared war on Nazi Germany. Cardington was to be his first base.

My Parents

Phillip & Florence's wedding day, May 6th, 1939.

Shadows of the Past

It made me very proud to hear that friends of my father found him to be at all times a gentleman, a quiet man always ready to help anyone in need. He was to me, as both a child and then a young man, firstly a disciplinarian, very keen on such things as cleaning teeth, washing behind your ears, polishing shoes, etc. A good provider for the family, we always seemed to have enough to go round, but no seconds. He enjoyed the simple things in life, such as his pipe or the odd cigar, a glass or two of perhaps whisky or beer.

It was at the table that he was most disciplined and we all, my brother, two sisters and I, had to hold our knives and forks properly with the handles firmly in the palm of our hands. We would, when finished, place our knives and forks together centrally on our plates and sit up straight; no leaning on the table!

Father was meticulous when eating and it was almost a ritual to spread butter and marmalade on his toast. I remember watching him time and time again preparing his food for eating (possibly as a direct result of having gone without food in Yugoslavia). Nevertheless, he was an excellent father and as I grew up I came to respect and love him very much. I was 33 years old when he died, and for many years afterwards carried an enormous chip on my shoulders. Father was 59 when he died and as I write this I am 56, so when he passed away, he was not an old man and should have been looking forward to a period in life when he would be financially sufficient and unwind to a relaxed way of life, retirement being not far away. I suppose now, even after 26 years, I still have this chip on my shoulder, but it's not quite so big. The usual thing that comes to mind is 'Why? My father did more than his share for this country during the war and didn't deserve to die so painfully and prematurely. Well, I know some might think that this is not the way to think, but I do.

When I look back to my years at home, my Mum was a homemaker and always mending socks or knitting scarves and jumpers. An excellent cook, Mum always had a very tasty table. Every day meat and two vegetables were followed by a sweet, treacle sponge and custard being my favourite. Father always appreciated his food. After returning to England from Nazi occupied Yugoslavia, where going without regular

Shadows of the Past

meals and eating very basic foods, food had a new meaning and probably set the pattern of appreciation for the rest of his life.

Although father played no team games, he was for a short time an amateur boxer. He loved football and cricket and was a keen Leicester City and Tigers, and county cricket supporter. Together we watched many Leicester City home games at the kop end and we both enjoyed the atmosphere and colourful individuals who make an afternoon's football so much more enjoyable.

Later in my teens, I remember being introduced to the game of golf by my father. For a while I enjoyed the father/son companionship, finding that golf requires long periods of time. I soon found that wanting to follow all the other pursuits of a young man left no time for golf. I loved competition shooting and this I found plenty of in the Territorial Army (4/5th Battalion the Royal Leicestershire Regiment, nicknamed 'The Tigers').

Father was always very interested and followed the progressing inventions in aeronautics. The America v Russia Space Race was followed with particularly eager enthusiasm.

In 1975, however, he tragically contracted cancer of the stomach, and after an operation to try to stem the disease it was apparent that he probably would not live for much longer. On June 8th, 1976 he passed away. He was a member of the RAFA club at Wigston Magna, where he had helped to organise the branch meetings and social functions at the Royal British Legion Club. He was given a forces burial, the coffin draped with the Union Jack. I remember following the hearse with my father's coffin draped with the flag and seeing a passing policeman stand to attention, saluting the passing entourage. This moment gave me an unforgettable feeling.

These, then, are but brief recollections of my father, a man who I remember wanted to work and earn enough to support a family, and who deserved, but did not get, time to enjoy watching his children and grandchildren grow up.

Early Memories

My earliest recollections of my father's RAF service were during my early years, somewhere between the ages of seven to 10. I was aware that at weekends he disappeared somewhere and found out that he was an RAF reservist, and as such carried out his pilot training at Desford airfield, Leicestershire (No 7 RFS); he would go for training twice a month.

A Tiger Moth flown by Tubby at Desford, June 11th, 1950.

One of his regular instructors was Squadron Leader Bullimore, quite a character and an exceptional instructor, he was known as 'Bats' Bullimore - not because he was 'batty', but because he was brilliant at aerobatics. In 1934, he had flown an Avro 504K with Sir Alan Cobham's famous air circus. During these training flights, airfields such as Moreton, Sywell and Donnington, amongst many others, would be visited and then he would return home to Desford. I can remember on many occasions my mother informing my brother, sisters and I that our dad would be flying over our house at about 2 pm. Mum would tell a few near neighbours of Tubby's approximate arrival time, so by the time Dad was due, there were many people standing in their gardens with tea towels at the ready to wave to him. The houses were built back-to-back and Kingston Avenue was about 400 yards long with Burley Avenue adjacent, the reception committee consisted of approximate 60 people for the first flypast. As 2 pm approached, sure enough we could hear the drone of the aircraft and a Tiger Moth then appeared. I am not sure what the safe height was for flying, maybe 200-300 feet. Certainly no more, but I could certainly see my father very clearly smiling and waving. Usually we had two flypasts

Shadows of the Past 17

and hearing the first one, dozens of people, mainly children, would come out to wave to Dad, who by this time was turning around to carry out his second run. Standing with my friends, I would tell them with pride that it was my dad flying the aircraft. These happy childhood times are firmly fixed in my mind and still give me great pleasure.

Desford Christmas

Some of my happiest memories are of the Christmas parties at Desford airfield. Every Christmas brought its children's party, this was looked forward to very much by all the family - Christmas with snow is always special and one Christmas it did snow, not a lot, but snow in any quantity is wonderful for children. The main party room was, I believe, either the Sergeants' or Officers' Mess. The building was fronted by the airfield and runway, which was grassed. After the party food had been swiftly eaten, the front glass doors of the room would be opened and all the children, with their coats on, went outside to look for Father Christmas, who would arrive, I believe, in an Avro Airspeed Oxford. The aircraft would taxi from the other side of the airfield; it was usually dusk about 3 or 4 pm. The aircraft would stop immediately opposite our building and Father Christmas would step out and down the steps with his large sack to the waiting children. With its engines still running, the aircraft then taxied away into the night. This was wonderful to me, and I would tell all my friends about having seen Santa arrive by aeroplane. Everyone received a present out of Santa's sack, and being too interested in the presents and party games, no one noticed as Santa slipped away to carry out his other Christmas duties!

RAF Desford Xmas Party: my sister, Ann, in the white dress, myself immediately above her left shoulder, & my eldest sister, Christine, immediately left of Santa's sack.

Chapter One

The Civil Air Guard

The formation of the Civil Air Guard in 1938/39 brought flying within reach of almost all pockets, so the CAG consequently played a significant part in Britain's preparation for war

On March 11th, 1938, Germany marched into Austria, her policy of rearmament and open aggression against her neighbours now evident to the entire world. She had already set foot on the patch, which was to lead to the Munich Crisis, the occupation of Czechoslovakia and World War Two.

Meanwhile, in this country, the situation had certain similarities with that of later years. In the country as a whole and in the Labour Party particularly, although facts stared them in the face, many refused to believe in the possibility of World War Two and looked to peace through disarmament - peace, in fact, at any price. The result was that whilst endless debates on rearmament took place in the House of Commons, little was being done either way.

Tubby, in CAG uniform, well on the way towards becoming a pilot, in his father's garden, Countesthorpe.

So far as the RAF was concerned, although production lines had been laid down for the Hawker Hurricane and Supermarine Spitfire, front line fighters were still, in the main, biplanes with fixed-pitch propellers and fixed undercarriages, whilst for bombers, there were only Fairey Battles, Handley-Page Hampdens and Armstrong-Whitworth Whitleys. The performance of these machines all fell far short of those aircraft used by the *Luftwaffe*, which incorporated new techniques, developed in recent years in the United States. Civil aviation at the time was in much the same laggard state. This too came under the

Shadows of the Past

umbrella of the Air Ministry, through the Under Secretary of State for Air, who, by tradition, was responsible to and answered in Parliament for civil aviation.

In May 1938, as a result of criticism in the Cadman Report of the Air Ministry's handling of civil aviation and of the air estimates, the Secretary of State for Air, Lord Swinton, resigned and was replaced by Sir Kingsley Wood. At the same time, the Under Secretary of State, Colonel A J Muirhead, also moved on, his task passing to Captain Harold Balfour, an active pilot and Royal Flying Corps (RFC) survivor from the First World War (1914-18).

With the new appointments, a wind of change blew through the corridors of the Strand's Aerial House; Sir Kingsley Wood brought from the Post Office a reputation for getting things through the Treasury, but had no experience of aviation. It therefore fell to Balfour, with his wide experience as a pilot and director of Saunders Roe in the aircraft industry, to supply the drive and initiative necessary to waken the Air Ministry from its slumber. In the coming year, some of his drive was directed towards the setting up of an organisation called the Civil Air Guard and in this task, Balfour was particularly well supported by W P Hildred, Deputy Director-General of Civil Aviation (DDGCA), who Lord Swinton had recruited shortly before his departure to combat the alleged "lack of energy and leadership" with which Cadman had charged the civil side of the Air Ministry.

The major difference between the British scheme and those of Italy, Germany and Russia was that it was voluntary. In other countries, the young were being conscripted. Here, all that was asked of those who joined was that in a national emergency, they would serve in the RAF or another branch of aviation, in whatever capacity was required. There was no obligation on the part of the authorities to employ them as pilots, for this, they must join the RAFVR.

The Civil Air Guard scheme came into effect on September 1st, 1938. Flying was not to start however, until October 1st. This gave the clubs a breathing space in which to build up their fleets, hire additional instructors and generally be organised to meet the new requirements. Only one

Shadows of the Past

sour note sounded and that was the next step forward, so far as the CAG scheme was concerned, in January 1939: it was announced that 'A' Licence holders were each to be put into one of four grades according to their age and the part they could be called upon to play in war. 'Class A1' was to consist of males between the ages of 18 and 30 who might be expected to join the RAF as operational pilots. 'Class A2' consisted of men over 30 with exceptional instructional or general flying experience who might be suitable to the RAF as either pilots or instructors.

Those in the age group 30-40 who, for age or medical reasons, were not eligible for Class A were to be put in 'Class B' and would be liable for call-up in the RAF as observers, air gunners, wireless operators, etc. The last class, 'C', was reserved for men who did not fall into any of the above categories and all women CAG members. These, according to experience, it was envisaged could be used as civilian ambulance or ferry pilots or for general communications duties. Those who did not qualify for any of these classes would be recommended to take up some form of national service. Within each group, members were to be classified further by means of a 'starring' system, those 'starred' being allocated some additional flying. Starred members of Class A1 would be required to attend travelling RAF Medical Boards and if passed fit would be allotted a further 10 hours CAG flying and some advanced training, after which they would be tested by the RAF. Starred members of Class A2 would also get extra CAG flying, but would not, for the time being, have to take a medical or be tested. Starred members of Class B would get extra CAG flying, would be tested and would be given extra training in the form of lectures and special instruction in the duties for which they had been selected, whilst in Class C, although some in this group would also be selected, they would get no further flying or instruction. Those starred in the various groups would, it was said, be able to wear special gold stars. The women, needless to say, were not at all happy about being thrown en bloc into Class C and thus being ineligible for further training.

In June 1939, when a review was being taken of CAG members available for RAF call-up, it was noted that there were some 800 to 900 women members, 200 of which had qualified as pilots. These, especially the more experienced ones, together with the women instructors, were becoming more and more restless about the lack of information as to how they might be used in war and the Air Ministry discussion continued about how, if any were to be used as ferry pilots, they would be organised. Flying Training was to be carried out at local flying clubs.

The Civil Air Guard 1938-39

The new Secretary of State for Air, Sir Kingsley Wood, announced the formation of the Civil Air Guard on July 23rd 1938. Members of the public aspiring to become pilots were invited to apply to 76 clubs for training. All of these clubs had agreed to participate in the scheme - probably due to the attractive scale of payments offered by the government for the use of the club's aircraft, instructors, engineers and premises. Tubby Gaunt was to train at Leicestershire Aero Club, Braunstone, and was one of the aspiring flyers.

The CAG did not actually own any aeroplanes or premises. The clubs were paid £30 for each pupil who qualified for a licence, £50 if on heavier aircraft, with payments for up to 10 hours annual practice flying after qualification. As the scheme developed, so the clubs sought additional machines to provide for the extra needs of CAG flying.

A club had to have a CAG section of a minimum of 12 pupils before commencing training. Men and women applicants aged between 18 and 50, medically fit and free of any military reserve commitment, would be taught to fly at a cost to them of 2/6d (12½p) per hour during the week and 5/-d (25p) at weekends and public holidays on aircraft under 1,200 lbs (544 kgs) all-up-weight. Above this weight (on types such as the DH Moth) the charges were doubled. The normal club charge at the time was £1.10.0d (£1.50) per hour. By joining the scheme, the applicants undertook to offer themselves for service, which would not necessarily involve flying, in a national emergency. A basic uniform was provided, this being a pale blue boiler suit with buttoned breast pockets and a matching belt. A miniature civil aviation ensign with the letters 'CAG' superimposed was worn on the shoulders. Members were required to join their club operating the scheme for a much reduced membership fee. On qualifying as a pilot, a pair of 'wings' with 'CAG' in the centre was worn above the breast pocket.

Shadows of the Past

A committee was appointed to administer the scheme as follows: -
<u>Chief Commissioner</u>
The Most Hon the Marques of Londonderry, KG, PC, MVO
<u>Hon Secretary</u>
Air Cdre John A Chamier, CB, CMG, DSO, OBE, RAF (Ret'd)
<u>Hon Area Commissioners</u>
W Lindsay Everard, MP (Knighted in 1939)
Maj. Alan Goodfellow, RAF (Ret'd)
Mrs F G Miles
Robert Murray, Esq.

Of the original 76, only 58 clubs actually operated the scheme, and training started in September 1938. By the following January, 5,500 of the original 30,000 applicants had been accepted and already 1,380 of these had gained their 'A' licences and thereby qualified to wear the CAG flying brevet. These figures illustrate the pace of instruction at the clubs during the autumn. These statistics do not include normal club instruction, which continued simultaneously with CAG flying. For this hard work, the clubs were paid £40,823. By the time the scheme ended, there were over 10,000 members, of whom more than 7,000 had qualified.

On January 24th 1939, the scheme was categorised for the various age groups. Those up to 30 or 40, if having special qualifications, formed a special pilot reserve; those between 30 and 40 were to be available for secondary flying duties; and the third category contained the remainder and all women.

Many members served in the air during the war, either in the armed forces or in the Air Transport Auxiliary (ATA). Had it not been for the additional strength of the Auxiliary Air Force (AAF), it is possible that the Battle of Britain would have been lost. Without the CAG, the ferry organisation would have been hard pressed to cope with the delivery of aircraft from the factories and thus make good the losses.

One Pilot an Hour

Statistics show that the CAG was training one pilot to 'A' Licence standard every hour of daylight.

Shadows of the Past 23

During the long days of midsummer, it is estimated that the output of pilots was increased to the point of training one pilot an hour for every hour in the 24, a rate of 9,000 a year.

The CAG movement was achieving three important objects: it was creating a large body of men and women with a practical knowledge of flying, which would be useful in any emergency; by broadening the basis of entry into aviation, it helped to make the average citizen air-minded and fully conscious of the vast potentialities of the air; further, it helped to increase the numbers of those who found employment in aviation, whether as pilots, ground engineers, or on the constructional side of the aircraft industry.

A civilian 'A' Licence, however, was no substitute for a service flying training course, so many CAG members volunteered for other aircrew categories. One such, W Cutting of the West Suffolk Aero Club CAG, was an air gunner in a Whitley on operations, when the aircraft's pilot was killed. Although he had only flown Taylor-craft aeroplanes before, he now took control of the twin-engined, 21,660 lbs (9,825 kgs) bomber and flew it back to base, thus saving both the valuable crew and the aircraft. For this, he was awarded the Distinguished Flying Cross. The cost to him of his CAG training had been under £5, but the value to the country of his bravery far exceeded the small subsidy paid for his pilot training. This is but one example of the way in which the country gained from the CAG scheme.

A delightful photo of all three brothers, Maurice, Arthur & Phillip, at Maurice & Tilly's wedding. November 14th, 1940. Note the diagonal blast tapes on windows at rear.

Chapter Two

The Training Starts

After signing the respective papers on volunteering to join the RAFVR in Leicester, on September 2nd, 1939, Tubby's first posting was RAF No.2 Receiving Centre at Cardington, Bedfordshire, on November 10th, 1939. Within a few days, on November 15th, Tubby was posted to No.8 receiving centre at Manston, where he was to undergo his basic training, which was to take six weeks. Issued with his kit, Tubby quickly settled down to forces living and discipline, mixing easily. He quickly found new friends, having a photograph taken with six of such outside their billet; each airman signed the back of all seven copies for future reference.

Manston, December 3rd, 1939. Tubby is far left, Cliff Ginnette rear left, G. Haddon far right. These seven friends all signed the photo; by September 1941, four are either missing or dead.

It would not be long before the grim realities of war became evident. Almost 12 months to the day after the photograph was taken, the first of four of his comrades were killed in action, this including G. A. Hadden. Some four months later, Sergeant Clifford Ginnette w/op & air gunner serving with 22 Squadron on Bristol Beauforts, was killed in action whilst attacking shipping in the Channel on April 24th, 1941. On July 5th, Sergeant Gerald Hutson, another w/op & air gunner, was killed in action with 106 Squadron flying in a Hampden from Coningsby

Shadows of the Past

in Lincolnshire. One month later, on August 26th, 1941, Sergeant Thomas Parkinson of 21 Squadron, Watton, Norfolk, was killed in action; this was to set the trend for Tubby's personal chances of survival.

From Manston, Tubby was posted to SHQ Debden, to the Signal & Wireless School. On January 26th, 1940, he was to begin his aircrew training as a w/op & air gunner, firstly successfully completing his classroom wireless training. On the move again to 51 Group, Tubby was classed as 'satisfactory to good'. Moving in quick succession, Tubby arrived at Cranwell (No 1 Signals School). Training here was to be carried out using Westland Wallace, Percival Proctor and Vickers Valencia aircraft. Flying training times varied from 10 minutes to over an hour. Successfully completing his wireless training, his Morse Code was acceptable at 18 words a minute receiving and 20 words a minute sending. Moving on again, Tubby was posted to No 4 Bombing & Gunnery School (B&GS) at West Frough. There he quickly learnt to handle and fire machine-guns and was passed as 'above average', this course being the last of his initial training, lasting some six weeks.

No 14 OTU Cottesmore, in Rutland, was to give Tubby familiarisation with both the Hampden bomber and working as an aircrew member. The Hampden was the aircraft that he was to fly in during his first tour of operations with 49 Squadron. This is also where he was to meet many of his flying comrades, in particular Sergeant Pilot Terry Freeman, with whom he would fly many of his operations over enemy occupied Europe with 49 Squadron from Scampton.

The early training and familiarisation on becoming a w/operator & air gunner at 14 OTU was carried out in Avro Ansons, then Hampdens and Vickers Wellingtons. Most of his pilots were Polish instructors: Squadron Leader Bukdwiski, Flying Officer Srymonski and Sergeant Gruszlznski, to name but a few. Tubby completed his course at Cottesmore on May 23rd, 1941. An interval posting to 'B' Flight as Staff Operator was to keep him busy until his transfer to 49 Squadron, with which he completed his first tour of active operations against the enemy.

Shadows of the Past
No 5 Group, 49 & 83 Squadrons, RAF Scampton

Just three miles north of Lincoln's magnificent cathedral lies Scampton airfield. This was a new airfield in 1938, and home to No 3 Group, but in quick succession was taken over by 5 Group and housed 49 and 83 squadrons, right through most of the war until 1944. It is perhaps the most potent symbol of the county's deep affiliation with the RAF, being as it is today not only an operational RAF air base but also home of the RAF'sfamous 'Red Arrows'. Back in 1938, with war on the horizon, the new Hampden bomber came into service with Scampton's two squadrons.

Within six hours of the declaration of war, at 11am on September 3rd, 1939, by Chamberlain's solemn words, nine aircraft, three from 49 and six from 83 Squadrons, took part in their first operation of the war. Accompanied by a further nine aircraft from 44 Squadron at Waddington, the operation was an offensive sweep over the entrance to the Kiel Canal, close to Wilhelmshaven, to attack the German pocket battleships there. The secondary target was the ammunition depot at Marienof, and on no account was anyone to attack civilian establishments. This token raid pushed through, found all aircraft taking off about 6 pm, reaching the target area late evening. The cloud dropped down to 300 feet and consequently unable to make contact with the enemy ships, the operation was aborted. Most of the crews had not flown at night, so navigation lights were switched on to keep all the aircraft together. Everyone experienced all the emotions and tension of their first operation and not being able to see, let alone attack, the enemy was very frustrating for all the crews.

The three aircraft from 49 Squadron were piloted by (L4040) Flight Lieutenant G.F. Lerwill, (L3046) Flying Officer RAB Learoyd and (L4093) Sergeant T P Pratt (later, on August 12th/13th, 1940, Learoyd was awarded the Victoria Cross for his 'signal act of valour' in pressing home his attack on the Dortmund - Eams Canal).

Of the 11 Hampdens, which included five from 83 Squadron and five from 49 Squadron in the attacking force, two failed to find the target, four carried out diversional attacks, only the five remaining aircraft attacking the primary target. Under intense enemy fire, Flight Lieutenant P T Cairn-Hill and crew of 83 Squadron went in first and, although very badly shot up, dropped their bombs on target. The second and third attacks were made by 83 Squadron crews, but both were shot out of the sky, crashing close to the target. The fourth to attack was Pilot Officer Mathews and crew of 49 Squadron, pushing forward and being repeatedly hit by flak: with one engine stopped, they bombed the target successfully; Mathews brought his aircraft back to Scampton on one engine.

Learoyd and crew of 49 Squadron, witnessing the previous attacks, met the full force of the German defences head on, blinded by searchlights, the pilot brought his aircraft down to 150 feet above the canal, totally ignoring the onslaught of deadly cannon shells. The aircraft was repeatedly hit and large pieces of main planes were torn away. Completely blinded by the searchlights, he asked the navigator to guide him over the target, this was carried out with precision and the delayed action bomb which was fitted with a parachute, allowed the crew to locate the point of impact. The bomb hit the aqueduct and along with other hits, the target was destroyed.

Roderick Learoyd was one of six RAF VCs to survive the Second World War. Tubby was to meet him at No.14 OTU, while doing a stint as Staff Wireless Operator; Learoyd was the Commanding Officer (CO), indeed, Tubby's logbook bears the VC's signature.

By early 1941, Scampton had become one of the largest bomber airfields in the country; its two squadrons operating a total of 52 Hampdens and approximately 2,500 servicemen, who lived either in or around the airfield, many in tents before more suitable accommodation was built. The situation was to become worse in the autumn, with 5 Group's Target Marking Flight joining them, and which remained at Scampton throughout the winter months.

In the first two years of war, the Scampton squadrons lost over 150 Hampdens. By early spring, the first Manchesters arrived, signalling the end of operations for the obsolete Hampdens.

Shadows of the Past

Tubby's first flight in a Manchester was on April 2nd, 1942. He was wireless operator, the pilot being Wing Commander Stubbs, who was 49 Squadron's new CO. For Tubby, this month was to see him crewing for all the 'top brass' on 49 Squadron whilst awaiting orders for pilot training, which subsequently took him to Marshal's at Cambridge.

To be a bomber crew member required persistent fortitude in circumstances when the stoutest mind and heart would have every excuse to show a natural normal weakness. The average operation was in darkness and in the early hours of the morning. Berlin was the furthest target; Tubby's log shows 9 hrs l5mins, Cologne 6 hrs, with most of this time being over enemy occupied Europe. Everyone who took part in it knew that casualties were so high that the odds were against the survival of any particular airman. It never was and never could be a mode of warfare to be conducted in hot blood; the Bomber crews were engaged throughout the flight in a series of intricate tasks resembling those of a skilled craftsman. Calculations and minute adjustments of machinery had to be made all the time, with a clear head and steady hand. A long flight by night is in itself no task for the feint-hearted, when a small navigational error may result in a forced landing at best. All this had to be carried out in the face of the most formidable air defences. Searchlights and anti aircraft guns set up a visible and terrifying barrier between the bomber and the target. The far more deadly night fighters might at any moment during the flight of hundreds of miles over enemy territory, strike without warning, engaging for only two or three seconds, striking terror into the aircrews. In all encounters, bomber aircraft were at a gross disadvantage, with inferior speed manoeuvrability and firepower. How the young men flying the bombers coped with the inhuman strain and stress beggar's belief.

Chapter Three

Nos 49 & 83 Squadrons, No 5 Group

No 5 Group

With headquarters first at Grantham and later at Morton Hall, just off the Fosse Way by Swinderby, No 5 Group of RAF Bomber Command not only contributed to the general heavy bomber offensive, but was responsible for many of the most dramatic and specialised attacks of the war. These included the successive breaching of the Dortmund-Ems canal; the destruction of the Vohne and Eder dams and of the great Kembs dam on the upper Rhine; and the sinking of the capital battleships, *Tirpitz* and the *Lützow*. The famous daylight raid on the MAN diesel engine factory at Augsburg was also made by this Group, as were the big attacks on German cities and oil installations.

Many new weapons were launched on the enemy from aircraft based in southern Lincolnshire - the 12,000 lb earthquake bomb and the newer 22,000 lb monster, for instance. It is a far cry from the huge 10 tonners to the 250 and 500 lbs bombs, which were standard at the outbreak of war.

No 5 (Bomber) Group was formed during the RAF's 'Expansion Period' at Mildenhall on July 1st, 1937. On October 2nd the same year, they replaced HQ 23 Group at St Vincent's, Grantham, remaining there until November 14th, 1943, when they moved to their final home, Morton Hall, at Swinderby.

September 1939 found No 5 Group with HQ at Grantham (as mentioned above) and 10 squadrons spread over five stations: Scampton, Waddington, Hemswell, Finningley and Cottesmore. All squadrons were equipped with Hampden aircraft and six were still within the Group on VE-Day, May 8th, 1945: they were Nos. 49, 83, 44, 50, 61 and 106 Squadrons at Syerston, Coningsby, Spilsby, Skellingthorpe (50 and 61) and Metheringham respectively.

Shadows of the Past

Only one of the original five stations, Waddington, was contained in the Group at the end of European hostilities. At that time there were 12 stations and 18 Squadrons. Each squadron was capable of despatching some 20 to 25 aircraft for a really big raid. Thus from this one Group in south Lincolnshire alone, Air Chief Marshal Sir Arthur Harris could launch some 350 aircraft carrying close on 2,000 tons of high explosives against the enemy. Contrast those figures with the minute compiled by a group staff officer in February 1942, recording his pleasure that 'this group alone dropped no less than 19 tons of bombs on Mannheim last Wednesday'!

On September 14th, 1939, Air Vice-Marshal A T Harris, OBE AFC assumed command of No 5 Group. The future Air Officer Commanding-in–Chief RAF Bomber Command stayed with the Group for 14 months.

For the first six months of the war, the Group was engaged on North Sea sweeps, security patrols and leaflet raids. On January 11th, 1940, two aircraft from Waddington each dropped 324,000 leaflets on Hamburg and Bremen. Later that month, three aircraft from Scampton dropped leaflets over the Reich, but the first bombs to be released by the Group in anger were directed against the island of Sylt on the night of March 19th, 1940.

Then came the Norwegian campaign. The Group was kept busy but a grimmer note now began to appear. Where 'None of our aircraft is missing' had been a happy regularity, many familiar faces began disappearing from the Lincolnshire stations. For example, on April 12th, one of the Waddington squadrons sent five aircraft to attack enemy shipping in Kristiansund harbour: only one returned and that aircraft owed its escape to the wireless operator, Acting Corporal J Wallace, who removed the gun (fixed to fire only to the rear of the aircraft) from its mounting and shooting down two enemy fighters which were attacking from the beam. Later, as a Flight Lieutenant, he shared with Acting Corporal Caldecott, from the same station, the honour of being the first NCO in the Group to receive the Distinguished Flying Medal.

Bombs fell on Germany proper in mid-May of the same year, when a crossroads near Munchen-Gladbach was among the targets attacked in the Ruhr and at Hamburg. One squadron reported that flak was 'accurate at 2,000 feet over Hamburg". The Group was later to attack from more than 10 times that height.

The Battle for France in 1940, found the Group occupied with much the same duties they fulfilled between 'D' and 'VE' Days - support of troops in the field bombing German factories and synthetic oil plants and the laying of mines in the enemy's sea-lanes.

Whilst the Battle of Britain was being bitterly fought out, British bombers were striking at the heart of Germany (*see first raid). Berlin was attacked twice in August 1940. Invasion barges in enemy-held ports were a first priority target while the enemy also was attacking local airfields.

In the same month, Flight Lieutenant Learoyd, who was stationed at Scampton, was awarded the Victoria Cross for his daring lone attack on an aqueduct of the Dortmund-Ems canal. On the dive down to the aqueduct, the aircraft encountered intense light flak, which did considerable damage. After completing the attack from a height of only 150 feet, the aircraft turned and flew straight into a cluster of searchlights, which temporarily blinded the pilot. According to the wireless operator, the aircraft was then so low that the trees masked the enemy fire around the target.

Scampton earned another VC. the next month, awarded to Sergeant Hannah, regarding whose actions 'Bomber' Harris, who was still in command of No 5 Group, said "I consider that this is one of the clearest examples of most conspicuous bravery and extreme devotion to duty in the presence of the enemy under the most harassing conditions that I have come across".

At this time, people in the Boultham, Skellingthorpe district of Lincoln were taking an interest in a large wood clearance scheme in the area, which was to be absorbed by Skellingthorpe aerodrome. The preservation of the maximum amount of the wooded area made this one of the most charming airfields in the country (it was closed on November 15th, 1947). In order to make Waddington fit for heavy bombers to use, a large stretch of the Lincoln, Sleaford road was closed to the public. Airfields were

Shadows of the Past

also under construction, or were planned, at Syerston, Coningsby, Woodhall Spa and Bardney. Soon too, the powers hoped to bring the drone of heavy bombers to the people of East Kirkby, Spilsby and Strubby. All these stations, with those at Metheringham, Balderton and Fulbeck, were under the command of the AOC. No 5 Group at the close of the heavy bomber offensive from bases on 'aircraft carrier England'.

The Group began to convert from Hampdens to Manchesters in the summer of 1942 and where 250 lb and 500 lb bombs had been carried, one and two thousand pounders were being loaded into the bomb bays. Soon these were to be joined by 4,000 lb 'Cookies' and 8,000 lb 'Blockbusters'.

In March and April of 1941, the Group played its part in the daring daylight attacks on the *Scharnhorst* and *Gneisenau* at Brest (and later night raids in January 1942) - then the most heavily defended target in the world. On the night of October 12th/13th 1941, the Group recorded with pride that 118 aircraft were despatched to attack Huls and Bremen. It was their biggest effort up to then. In December, aircraft from this Group laid the smoke screen for the Commando raid on Vaagso Island.

Early in 1942, service and civilian people in Lincolnshire towns and villages were talking about a strange new airborne monster with four engines in place of the usual two and with characteristic twin fins and rudders: the Avro Lancaster had come to Lincolnshire.

The very first operation undertaken by Lancasters was on the evening of March 3rd 1942, when four set course from Waddington to lay mines in the Heligoland Bight. On the same night, Hampdens and Manchesters attacked the Renault works at Billancourt, near Paris. Later in March, the Group took part in the devastation raid on Lubeck.

Bomber Command was on the up and up!

The most sensational raid of the war up to then took place in daylight on April 17th, when 12 Lancasters, six from Waddington and six from Coningsby, let by Squadron Leader J D Nettleton (of Waddington's 44 Squadron), flew at tree-top height to attack the MAN diesel-engine factory

Shadows of the Past

*Scampton operations aircraft, AE187, 'OL-L', of 83 Sqn, shot down over Holland, September 1st, 1'941.
Photo by Doug Garton via Trevor Stocks.*

at Augsburg. The formations encountered fierce fighter opposition soon after crossing the French coast, but the attack was pressed home and resulted in severe damage on which was laid the very highest importance.

Squadron Leader Nettleton received the VC; only five of the 12 aircraft returned.

May 1942, brought the first of the 1,000 bomber raids, the target Cologne. No 5 Group contributed 162 aircraft and 286 tonnes of bombs. For his part in the attack, Flying Officer Manser, a pilot stationed at Swinderby, was awarded a posthumous VC. Before reaching the target, his aircraft was coned by searchlights and became a target for accurate flak. He went on and bombed from 7,000 feet while under fire. In his efforts to shake off the ground defences, he went as low as 1,000 feet over the target, but was not successful and one of his two engines was hit and put out of action. He managed to climb 2,000 feet in an effort to get back to this country, but while still over Belgium, was forced down to only 800 feet. He ordered the crew to bale out, but refused to leave the controls. His crew saw the plane go down in flames immediately afterwards.

Shadows of the Past

In September 1942, the Group's monthly tonnage of bombs passed the 2,000-ton mark for the first time.

During the eight days from October 17th to 24th, No.5 Group, unaided, made three of the most memorable raids in the history of Bomber Command.

On the 17th, 88 Lancasters, without fighter escort, flew deep into Central France to destroy the Schneider works at Le Creusot in daylight.

On the night of the 22nd, in preparation for the celebration of the fascist march on Rome, 86 Lancasters of No 5 Group flew to Genoa and delivered the most concentrated attack yet achieved without the loss of a single aircraft.

On the 24th, 73 Lancasters flew in daylight to Milan, where they wrought tremendous destruction with their 4,000 lb bombs.

February 1943 was another month of outstanding achievements - for the first time the Group's total sorties passed the 1,000 mark.

At 0056 hours on May 17th 1943, Wing Commander Guy Gibson, commanding the new Scampton squadron designated No 617, reported by radio to HQ that the Mohne Dam had been breached. Great damage was done. Powerhouses were put out of action and many roads, railways and bridges swept into the Ruhr and Eder Valleys. The Viaduct over the Ruhr carrying the railway from Hagen to Dortmund and the road bridge between Duisburg and Oberhausen were broken. Nineteen Lancasters made the attack, 11 of them returned.

The Squadron which effected this major triumph for No 5 Group had been especially formed some months before the attack, for which they engaged in special training - both in the air and on the ground. The personnel involved knew they were on something very special, but knowledge of the actual target was confined to just four officers in the entire Group. Following the success of this attack, No 617, the 'Dam Buster' Squadron, as they were to be known, moved from Scampton to Woodhall Spa; appropriately the unit's motto became 'Apres moi la deluge' ('After me came the flood').

Shadows of the Past

Other Lancasters in the Group at this time were taking a full part in the Battles of the Ruhr, of Cologne and of Hamburg.

One high spot of June 1943 again fell to No 5 Group, when 56 Lancasters from Bottesford, Langer, Fiskerton and Dunholme, led by Group Captain Slee DSO DFC, in command at Dunholme, embarked on a most ambitious programme. During the night of the 20th these Lancasters bombed Friedrichshafen, where not one of the principal buildings of the Zeppelin works escaped unscathed and some three acres of subsidiary workshops were devastated. The force then took the German defences completely by surprise by continuing their flight across the Alps to bases in North Africa. Three nights later, they made the return journey by way of Specia, where they delivered yet another damaging attack on the harbour and port installations.

In August 1943, this Group dropped no less than 5,838 tons of bombs; some of them on the V1 experimental station at Peenemunde, on the Baltic.

All through the winter that followed, Bomber Command fought in the Battle of Berlin. The city was mercilessly pounded from November 1943 to the spring of the following year.

49 Sqn, in front of an Avro Lancaster bomber, 1945.

In April 1944, all service leave was stopped and the magic word 'Invasion' was on everyone's lips. The Group's priority targets were enemy road and rail communications in France. These called for a high standard of bombing accuracy. This was greatly aided by a new system of marking the target which was largely evolved by Wing Commander Cheshire, of 617, the Dam Busting Squadron at Woodhall Spa. It was he who

Shadows of the Past

developed the Master Bomber idea and for his work in this respect, this bomber pilot was later to be awarded the VC.

June 6th, 1944, saw the long awaited 'D-Day', the Allied landings in Normandy. In this month, the Group flew more than 3,000 sorties for the first time in its history, but the news spotlight fell most brightly on aircraft operating from Woodhall Spa, which on June 8th, launched for the first time the 12,000 lb 'Earthquake' bomb. The target was the Saumer tunnel through which all direct rail communications from the South of France to the Normandy front had to pass. The complete destruction of this tunnel by a direct hit at its southern end was an outstanding achievement for the Group and a major blow to the enemy.

July was notable for the many attacks on flying bomb storage dumps and launching sites. Here again, 12,000 lb bombs were used with devastating effect.

August saw aircraft from Woodhall Spa, Bardney, and Metheringham attack the U-boat bases at La Pallice, Lorient and Brest. At Brest, the battleship, *Clemenoeau*, and the cruiser, *Gueydon*, were sunk, thus preventing the enemy from carrying out his intention of blocking the harbour. The Group also twice attacked Königsberg unaided. These were the longest bombing missions yet made by Lancasters and great damage was done to the Baltic port. As a result of two daring low-level mining efforts against the ships canals at Stettin and Könisberg, all Swedish shipping was withdrawn from the Baltic trade. Coningsby and Metheringham supplied the aircraft.

On September 15th, Lancasters from Woodhall Spa and Bardney made the first attack on the Tirpitz using 12,000 lb bombs. As a result, the great battleship was severely damaged. A week later, the Dortmund-Ems canal was breached for the first time by aircraft from Metheringham, Skellingthorpe, Waddington, Bardney and Woodhall. During September, Wing Commander Guy Gibson VC, flying as a Master Bomber for the first time since the attack on the dams, lost his life in the attack on Rheydt. On 19th/20th September 1944 Gibson's aircraft, a Mosquito, crashed in flames near the village of Steen-Bergen-En-Kruisland, 13 km north of Bergen Op-Zoom.

Aircraft from East Kirkby, Spilsby and Strubby played a large part in flooding Walcheren Island early in October, but the big news of the month was the destruction of the great Kerns Dam by aircraft from Woodhall. The crews who pressed home their attack - six of them, led by Wing Commander J B Tait DSO DFC, from only 600 feet, experienced intense light flak. The *Tirpitz* which had been moved from Alten Fjord to Tromso Fjord, was again attacked but there was too much cloud for accurate bombing.

An example of the high standard of bombing accuracy, which had now been achieved by the Group, was shown in their attacks on Brunswick in mid-October. In spite of many earlier attacks, this town had seemed to bear a charmed life. This time it was decided to finish the place, once and for all. Twelve squadrons were used and the Target Area was split up into six sections, each of which was to be attacked by a pair of squadrons. Target Indicator markers were dropped on the railway station. All squadrons were to use three markers, but each pair was to attack from a slightly different heading. Thus, aircraft from Skellingthorpe and Waddington attacked the Northern section; aircraft from Metheringham, Spilsby and Fulbeck attacked the North-Eastern area and aircraft from East Kirby, Strubby and Balderton shared the Eastern side of the town. Anyone who saw the newsreel film of this attack can have no doubt of its success and Brunswick was only one of the many towns to which No 5 Group gave its much specialised attention. The technique built up by this Group undoubtedly achieved results, which in terms of bombs per crew over the target area, are unsurpassed by any other bombing force in the world.

The *Tirpitz* was eventually sunk on November 12th by 29 aircraft from Woodhall Spa and Bardney, which made a round flight of over 2,200 miles.

Earlier in the month, No 5 Group had breached the Dortmund-Ems canal for the second time. Later, reconnaissance showed that repair work was well in hand. So yet, another attack was made. The Mittellland canal was also drained. To complete the month, the Group sent some 278 aircraft to attack Munich unaided. The weather was the worst in which

Shadows of the Past

any large bombing force had ever taken off. Cloud base was down to 600 feet and visibility was less than the length of the runways in use.

Mosquitoes from Woodhall celebrated New Year's Eve by a pinpoint attack by 12 aircraft on the *Gestapo* HQ in Oslo.

Early in January, Air Marshal Sir Ralph Cochrane KBE CB AFC, who had been in command of the Group for two years, left Morton Hall to take up the appointment of AOC-in-C Transport Command. His successor was Air-Vice Marshal HA Constantine, CBE DSO, until mid-October 1945, when he was followed by Air Commodore S C Elsworthy DSO DFC AFC (later Marshal of the RAF {MRAF} Sir Charles Elworthy CDS.).

The Dortmund-Ems and Mittelland canals were again breached on New Year's Day and again in February and March. For great gallantry in a blazing aircraft during the attack on New Year's Day, Flight Sergeant George Thompson, a wireless operator stationed at Bardney, was awarded the Victoria Cross posthumously.

A remarkable piece of pinpoint bombing was achieved on February 22nd, when 17 Bardney aircraft attacked and destroyed the viaduct at Altenbeken.

Outstanding achievement in March was the unaided bombing by No 5 Group of Wesel, immediately before Montgomery's Army crossed the Rhine on the night of March 23rd. Commandos captured the town that night with only 36 casualties. Field Marshal Montgomery said, "The bombing of Wesel last night was a masterpiece and was a decisive factor in making possible our entry into that town before midnight".

Before that, an aircraft from Woodhall Spa had carried the first 22,000 lb bomb to the Reich; this was on March 14th when the viaduct at Bielefeld was destroyed. Other bridges and viaducts destroyed by 22,000 lb and 12,000 lb bombs during March were those at Arnsberg, Arbergen, Nienburg, Bremen and Bad Oeynhausen. In all, this Group alone put seven bridges or viaducts out of action in 10 days.

Shadows of the Past

The effectiveness of the heavy bombing offensive became fully apparent only when the occupation of Germany became an accomplished fact.

After the end of the war, No 5 Group crews flew on many happier operations. Each day they brought back some thousands of liberated prisoners of war.

No history of the Group would be complete without mention of its fine record in the laying of mines in the enemy's waterways. No 5 Group were the pioneers, for it was from Scampton that the first mine-laying aircraft took off and for a long time, this Group alone looked after this vital job. The mining of the canal approaches to Stettin arid Königsberg has already been mentioned, but later on, Woodhall Mosquitoes penetrated far inland to mine the river Weser and the Kiel Canal.

No 5 Group was disbanded on 15 December 1945.

Chapter Four

49 Squadron, 'A' Flight – Scampton – No 5 Group

Tubby arrived at 49 Squadron on August 9th, 1941, being fully trained as a wireless op/air gunner. The next seven months would see Tubby participating in the early theatres of the bombing campaign over occupied Europe as part of aircrew, flying Hampden bombers.

Sorties included 'Gardening' operations (the laying of sea mines), the bombing of chemical installations along the Rhur Valley (known as 'Happy Valley') in Germany, attacking the German capital (battleships) in Brest Harbour (France), the *Scharnhorst* and *Prinz Eugen* and the intruder raids into designated areas, but selecting the targets at random, usually search light concentrations. Tubby spent three days settling in and experienced two flights to familiarize himself with the aircraft, the pilot being Pilot Officer McGuffie, who was sadly to be killed in action a year later.

First operation: bombing Brunswick, August 14th, 1941

Tubby's first operation was bombing Brunswick.

HAMPDEN AE132
P/O WALKER: pilot
P/O WOOD: navigator
Sgt CHEETHAM: wireless operator
Sgt GAUNT: air gunner
Up 2040 hrr, down 2350 hrs (3 hrs 10 mins)

Details of Sortie: -
Tubby's log book says returned early due to an unserviceable (US) engine.

It was not unusual to send new aircrew with the more experienced ones on their first operation. The operation proved disappointing for the crew. The aircraft suffered starboard engine failure, preventing it reaching the target.

Shadows of the Past 41

49 Sqn crest, 'Beware of the Dog'.

The summary of events for the raid on Brunswick gives an idea of how difficult it was to find and bomb a target using dead reckoning and visual means to reach and successfully bomb a given target during this early part of raids over occupied Europe.

Summary of Events: -
Weather - mainly cloudy, scattered showers and bright intervals. Visibility 8-12 miles.

24 aircraft to standby to bomb Brunswick GY4775, alternative S and M Germany, usual photo reconnaissance. All aircraft took off at short intervals and though only 11 aircraft were able to locate and bomb the primary objective owing to adverse cloud and haze, all remaining aircraft attacked alternative targets, Saldstedt, Hanover, Brunswick Town, Minden Leharte railway junction. Bremen, Arnham aerodrome and searchlight concentrations, in nine cases bursts were observed. Three aircraft overshot on landing and crashed without injury to crew. One aircraft AE 132 piloted by P/O Walker suffered a starboard engine failure, preventing it reaching the target.

The Bomber Command War Diaries (BCWD): -
Brunswick - 81 Hampdens to railway targets, one aircraft lost.

Second Operation: bombing Bremen, August 17th/18th, 1941

HAMPDEN AE132
P/O WALKER: pilot
Sgt WOOD: navigator
Sgt GAUNT: wireless operator & air gunner
Sgt CHEETHAM: air gunner
Up 2245 hrs, down 0535 hrs (6 hrs 50 mins)
(The operation saw P/O Wood again as navigator second pilot, to gain operational experience.)

Details of Sortie: -
Weather out was good, with considerable searchlight activity down to Bremen which was bombed at 0135. Had to use drastic avoiding action

Shadows of the Past 42

along the river Weser, until over the sea (although no reference is made why avoiding action taken, it would have almost certainly been enemy fighters). Tubby's logbook states that their aircraft was badly shot up.

Tubby (left) with two unknown airmen, possibly upon completion of training in January 1941.

Summary of Events: -
Weather - early mist, clearing - fine, with occasional low cloud.

13 aircraft to stand by to bomb Bremen GH484, alternatively the town. S and M last resort. 2 aircraft on special gardening operations, Pumpkin and Kraut. 2 gardeners took off and both ware successful in laying the mines as indicated, without incident. One aircraft landed at Coningsby on its return.

The 10 bombers took off at short intervals and only 4 claimed definite successes, owing to unfavourable weather and CU Cloud. Searchlight concentrations N.W of Bremen, Focke-Wulf works, S.W of town, Kiel, S.W Cuxhaven and Northolz aerodrome were the alternatives attacked by the remaining aircraft, 1 returning with its load. Few results were seen and all aircraft experienced accurate and intense flak on the target areas. Of the 59 aircraft despatched by bomber command, 2 Hampdens failed to return. All 49 squadron came home safely.

Shadows of the Past

Results: -

39 Hampdens and 20 Whitleys, with the Focke-Wulf factory and the railway goods station as aiming points. Hits were claimed on the Focke-Wulf factory, with two Hampdens lost.

At Scampton August 4th, 1941 - August 7th, 1942
Aircraft & Aircrew Losses between those dates

Target Dusseldorf: Collision Tragedy

Hampdens began returning to Scampton shortly after 0200 hrs on Monday, August 25th.

Because of recent intruder activity by German night-fighters around Hampden bases, our aircraft had elected not to use navigation lights whilst in the airfield circuit. It is not certain if this was the case on this particular morning, but whilst 49 and 83 Squadrons' aircraft (83 being the sister squadron to 49 at Scampton), were awaiting permission to land, H-Harry from 49 Squadron and F-Freddy of 83, hit each other over the village of Hackthorn to the north-east of Scampton airfield. The wreckage from both aircraft fell to the ground around Whale Jaw farm. Tragically there were no survivors. The accident was timed at 0250 hrs. Sergeant Owen McMahon, pilot of the 49 Squadron aircraft, is buried in Scampton churchyard, whilst his three fellow crew members were each returned to their respective hometowns for burial.

Scampton's night of anguish was sadly not yet over, for at 0400 hrs, as AE223 of 83 Squadron returned to dispersal from operations, the aircraft suddenly exploded killing all the crew and four ground crew members. It is thought that a wing bomb, which failed to release over the target, became dislodged when the aircraft landed and taxied back to its dispersal point. All 49's remaining aircraft returned safely.

Crashed AD967 (EAH)

Sgt O B McMAHON:	pilot	(killed)
Sgt E WELBOURNE:	wireless operator & air gunner	(killed)

Shadows of the Past

Sgt I D MaCKINNON: air gunner   (killed)
Sgt G F UPTON: 2nd pilot   (killed)

Third Operation: Intruding, Cologne, August 26th/27th, 1941
(Destroying Searchlights and Dropping Incendiaries)

HAMPDEN AD960
P/O. WALKER: pilot
Sgt WOOD: navigator
Sgt GAUNT: wireless operator & air gunner
Sgt CHEETHAM: air gunner
Up 2215 hrs, down 0610 hrs (7 hrs 55 min)

P/O Walker

Details of Sortie: -
No searchlights or flak on route south of Liege. Pinpointed position on Rhine through gaps in cloud, made several dive bombing attacks on searchlights and planted incendiaries in middle. Nice fire started with one stick. Tubby's log records 'badly shot-up'.

Summary of Events: -
Continuous rain and risk of low cloud and thunder. 11 aircraft to stand by, seven to bomb point B in area Cologne, alternatively the town. Four aircraft to act as intruders to attack searchlights belt on 10 mile sector, west of main target. Four further aircraft to lay mines in Nectarine. 14 aircraft took off at intervals, one returning shortly owing to engine trouble and 11 were successful (including the two gardeners). One aircraft suffered excessive oil temperature and low pressure and so before returning, bombed searchlights on enemy coast. Two bombers observed bursts and 1 took successful photographs. One attacked the estimated target on the intruder side - all were successful (from low altitudes) in causing searchlights to be extinguished. One Wellington and one Whitley failed to return from the operation; all 49 squadron came home safely.

Shadows of the Past 45

Results:-
99 aircraft consisting of 47 Wellington, 29 Hampdens, 22 Whitleys, one Manchester - to the city centre and to railway yards. Six further Hampdens made searchlight-suppression flights 10 miles west of Cologne, without loss. Good bombing was claimed in clear visibility. Cologne records indicate that most of the bombing was probably east of the city, with only about 15% of the bombs dropped being inside the city limits. 8 people were killed in Cologne. Two aircraft lost.

August 28th/29th, 1941

Eight aircraft sent from 49 Squadron on a searchlight suppression raid. Of these, two aircraft failed to return – Pilot Officer Bernard Fournier (AD971) and crew became victims of a night-fighter. At 330 hrs their aircraft fell in flames into the Waddenzee just south of the Isle of Ameland; there were no survivors. The 21 year old pilot and his crew are buried in Nes Cemetery, Ameland, Holland. It is believed that Pilot Officer Thomas Pratt (AE126) and crew also fell to the cannons of a night-fighter, they also came down in the Waddenzee and again, sadly, there were no survivors. The body of Sergeant Charles Hodkinson came ashore near Richel on September 8th. The following day the body of 25 year old Pilot Officer Pratt was found, Sergeant Arthur Willis also being washed ashore on September 10th, and two days later the body of Pilot Officer Harry Tongue was found near Vliehors.

Trevor Stocks, 1944-45 (wearing Air Gunner brevet).

Shadows of the Past
FTR AD971
P/O B M FOURNIER: pilot (killed)
Sgt D H BARRETT: navigator (killed)
F/S E R PALMER: wireless operator & air gunner (killed)
Sgt D WATSON: as above (killed)

FTR AE126
P/O T P PRATT: pilot (killed)
P/O H C TONGE: navigator (killed)
Sgt A C WILLIS: wireless operator & air gunner (killed)
Sgt HODGKINSON: as above (killed)

Trevor Stocks, 1940, when an 'Erk', standing at the left parachute-end, & Cpl Tam Murray standing on wheel fusing 2,000 lb mine as used on 'gardening operations. Sadly, Tam was killed in a fusing accident at this Bomb Dump in 1941.
Photo: Trevor Stocks

Fourth Operation: Bombing Frankfurt, August 29th/30th, 1941

HAMPDEN AD960
P/O WALKER: pilot
P/O WOOD: navigator
Sgt CHEETHAM: wireless operator & air gunner
Sgt GAUNT: air gunner
Up 2105 hrs, down 0520 hrs (8 hrs 15 mins)

Shadows of the Past

*Trevor Stocks & Cpl Tam Murray with a 2,000 lb armour piercing bomb, as used against the Scharnhorst, outside No 3 Hangar, 1940. Note the Hampdens to left of photo.
Photo: Trevor Stocks.*

Details of Sortie: -
8/10. 10/10 Cloud over whole trip, breaking up over Frankfurt. Impossible to identify actual target, but bombed light flak along river near centre of town, seen through gap in cloud.

Summary of Events: -
Weather mainly fair, with local showers and ground haze.

10 aircraft to stand by to bomb inland port at Frankfurt, alternative the town. Last resort as detailed in BCSO or built-up areas in Germany.

10 aircraft took off at short periods, but owing to almost 10/10 cloud, four aircraft were unsuccessful in locating the target and three were doubtful of success. Flak/Frankfurt town and an aerodrome (unidentified) were alternatives bombed. But only in one case were bursts seen. Generally, heavy icing was encountered, increasing the difficulties. Broomfield's crew (X3057) limped back across the sea with their aircraft's starboard engine repeatedly cutting out. After sending an SOS, the pilot eventually made a safe landing at Manston shortly after 0245 hrs.

Shadows of the Past

Results: -

143 aircraft, of which 73 Hampdens, 62 Whitleys, 5 Halifax and three Manchesters took part. This was the first 100 plus aircraft raid on this city, with railways and harbours as aiming points. The first sortie by an Australian squadron was flown in this raid, when Squadron Leader French and his crew took a 455 Squadron Hampden to Frankfurt and returned safely. Two Hampdens and one Whitley were lost. Bad weather prevented accurate bombing and crews reported that the attack became general in this Frankfurt area. Frankfurt reported that only light and scattered bombing took place, with damage to a gas works, a cask merchant's depot, and to several houses. Eight people were killed, seven of them in one house, which was struck by a bomb.

Honours & Awards

September 1941

F/S R Woolston	DFM
Sgt W L Donley	DFM
Sgt F Lowe	DFM
Sgt G Wood	DFM

October 1941

F/O R J Hannan	DFC
Sgt W A Bunn	DFM
Sgt J Leslie	DFM

November 1941

Sgt J Flint	DFM
S/Ldr A W Hiron	DFC
F/Lt H W H Fisher	DFC
P/O D B Falconer	DFC
Sgt A G Smith	DFM
Sgt B G Tree	DFM

Shadows of the Past

December 1941

F/O Scorer   DFC
Sgt D J P Broomfield   DFM
Sgt W C Samual   DFM

Squadron Strength, September 1ˢᵗ, 1941

'The posted strength of this Squadron 1 Sept. 1941 was as follows - 30 officers, 555 Airmen. Aircraft held by this unit were 24 Hampdens representing initial equipment, 3 Hampden aircraft representing reserve equipment, 1 Tiger Moth representing training equipment'.

Fifth Operation: Bombing Berlin, September 2ⁿᵈ/3ʳᵈ, 1941

HAMPDEN AD759
P/O GREEN: pilot
Sgt READ: navigator
Sgt GAUNT: wireless operator & air gunner
Sgt WARREN: air gunner
Up 1943hrs, down 0400 hrs (Fog – landed Driffield) (8 hrs 17 mins)

Details of Sortie: -
Weather 9-10 cloud, which helped against searchlights, as also did IFF (Identification: Friend or Foe). Ran in from South East and bombed with 250 lbs to draw fire, but this was unsuccessful. After further search, found gap in clouds and bombed with 1000 lbs a built up area and factory.

Summary of Events: -
16 aircraft to standby for operations, 12 to attack Berlin, one to attack Manheim, three to lay mines near Schiermonnikoog.

16 aircraft (including two gardeners) took off at short intervals and nine were successful in attacking main objectives (including one gardener). Being unable to locate the area owing to 10/10 cloud, the other gardener returned to base with the mines. Five other aircraft were unsuccessful, but bombed alternative targets - Neubahndenburgh, Stettin and Lubeck,

Shadows of the Past

also built-up areas. Four aircraft only observed results of bombing and on return, owing to intense fog in Lincolnshire, four aircraft crash landed at other dromes, without injury to crews. In eight other cases, landings were made at other dromes. Difficulties were encountered with A/A fire and in one case an Me I09 attacked and is believed shot down. Petrol shortage was experienced and also oxygen failure. Two Halifaxes, two Hampdens and one Manchester failed to return from Berlin and two Hampdens were reported missing from the mine-laying sorties.

Results BCWD: -
49 aircraft, which consisted of 32 Hampdens, seven Halifaxes, six Stirlings, four Manchesters. Five aircraft consisting of two Halifaxes, two Hampdens and one Manchester were lost. The Manchester loss contained the commanding officer of 615 Squadron, Wing Commander GE Valentine, and Group Captain JF Barrett, the Station Commander of North Luffenham. Both officers were killed and are buried in the Berlin War Cemetery.

Honours & Awards, August 1941.

Sgt A Donovan	DFM
Sgt P J N Lamb	DFM
Sgt J Flint	DFM
S/Ldr G R Trench	DFC

Aircraft & Crew Losses

Bombing Berlin & Keil, - September 7th/8th, 1941: -

Three aircraft from the unit were detailed to attack Kiel. Two completed their sorties and returned safely. Out of the 51 in total despatched against Kiel, three failed to return and one of these came from 49 Squadron. Tragically, 22 year old P/O John Bremham (AE236) and crew all perished and are buried in Kiel War Cemetery.

FTR AE 236
P/O J W T BROMHAM: pilot   (killed)
Sgt P J DUFFY: wireless operator & air gunner (killed)

Sgt E V DURHAM: 2nd pilot   (killed)
Sgt A KETTLEWORTH: wireless operator & air gunner (killed)

Sixth Operation: - Bombing Frankfurt, September 28th/29th, 1941

HAMPDEN AD759
P/O WALKER: pilot
SGT BLOCK: navigator
SGT MULLENGER: wireless operator
SGT GAUNT: air gunner
Up 2320 hrs, down 0615 hrs (6 hrs 55 mins)

This raid was a catastrophe from start to finish, with both appalling results and losses.

Details of Sortie: -
Failure of intercom on return. Glide attack from 14,000 feet to 10,000 feet. Bombed by light flare and burst observed in town. Flak moderate/heavy and accurate. Landed Detling on return. Weather abysmal. Returned to Scampton the next day at 1535 hrs, September 30th.

Summary of Events: -
Weather – east wind, local mist and fog. Dispersing at noon. Continuous rain late afternoon and local thunder.
2250 hrs - 14 aircraft to standby to bomb Frankfurt. Nine aircraft only took off, four being cancelled and one suffering a tail wheel collapse at the taxiing point. One aircraft cancelled at take off. One crashed eleven minutes after being airborne and all the crew were killed. One aircraft did not return from operations and nothing was heard of it (it later became known all the crew were taken prisoners and the cause of the crash has not been established). Five of the unit's aircraft landed at other aerodromes due to bad weather.

Crashed AE 376
Sgt WALKER: pilot   (killed)
Sgt A RAINE: wireless operator & air gunner (killed)
Sgt R E GREENHALGH: air gunner   (killed)
O/Bs Sgt T H SMITH: (killed)

Shadows of the Past

Failed to return AD 733
F/L J D Mundy DFC:	pilot (POW)
Sgt P C Darwin:	pilot (POW)
Sgt A Winton:	wireless operator & air gunner (POW)
F/S F Hibbert DFM:	as above (POW)

October was to be a busy month for Tubby and crews, four operations were carried out in a ten-day period. From a total of 99 aircraft sent to Bremen, two Wellingtons and one Hampden failed to return, all 49 Sqd aircraft returned. Of the 30 Hampdens and 14 Wellingtons despatched on the raid, one Wellington and one Hampden failed to return. Flight Lieutenant Mundy DFC (AD733) piloted the missing Hampden from 49 Squadron. The cause of this loss has never been established, but happily the crew survived to become POWs.

Seventh Operation: Bombing Bremen, October 12th, 1941

HAMPDEN AE132
P/O WOOD:	pilot
Sgt MACKEY:	navigator
Sgt GAUNT:	wireless operator & air gunner
Sgt POINTER:	air gunner

Up 1850 hrs, down 0150 hrs (7 hrs)

Details of Sortie: -
No cloud till German coast, 9/10 from there to target area, river observed by flare, presumed Weser, where heavy and light flak fired, so bombed concentration presumed Bremen.

(Again, this operation was not very successful.)

Summary of Events: -
Weather generally bright with cloudy periods and occasional rain.
16 aircraft to stand by, 12 to bomb objective at Huls and four to attack objective at Bremen. Four bombers took off to Bremen and none was successful in bombing main objective, owing to thick 10/10 clouds, which obscured target, concentration of flak and searchlights attacked in vicinity.

Shadows of the Past

P/O Wood (killed November 1941).

The flak was found to be intense. The remaining bombers took off and 11 were unsuccessful in bombing main objective. Two aircraft returned with bombs after two hours, owing to R/T (radio transmission) and engine trouble. One suffered excessive oil temperature. Seven aircraft bombed alternative targets - flak in the area - and three returned bombs to base. Heavy flak and thick cloud experienced by all, also several enemy aircraft were encountered.

Results BCWD: -
65 aircraft bombed in cloudy conditions and fires were seen.

Of the 99 aircraft dispatched to Bremen, two Wellingtons and one Hampden failed to return.

Eighth Operation: Bombing Cologne, October 13th/14th, 1941

HAMPDEN AE132
P/O WOOD: pilot
Sgt REID: navigator
Sgt GAUNT: wireless operator & air gunner
Sgt POINTER: air gunner
Up 0107 hrs, down 0722 hrs (6 hrs 15 mins)
Details of Sortie: -
On DR position Namur heavy Flak and concentration of searchlights observed three miles to port. Found Rhine and reached Cologne, but being unable to pinpoint railway yards, bombed town.

Summary of Events: -
Weather widespread mist and local fog becoming fair. Visibility poor, but improving later. Nine aircraft to stand by to bomb Cologne. At 0100

hrs, eight aircraft took off (one having a taxiing accident prior to take off and being unable to proceed). Four were successful in bombing main objective. Several aircraft experienced severe icing conditions and in one case an engine cut out on return, though a soft landing was made. One aircraft had a spin of 8000 feet owing to icing and on pulling out, the aileron controls were useless, necessitating forced landing on return. Two unsuccessful aircraft bombed areas in Cologne. No aircraft missing from this raid.

Results BCWD: -
30 Hampdens and nine Manchesters; Searchlight glare prevented target identification. Cologne reported only a few bombs. Six people killed, five injured and damage to 17 houses. No losses.

Ninth Operation: Bombing Duisberg, October 16th/17th 1941

HAMPDEN AE132
P/O WOOD: pilot
Sgt REID: navigator
Sgt GAUNT: wireless operator & air gunner
Sgt POINTER :   air gunner
Up 0037 hrs, down 0600 hrs (5 hrs 23 mins)

Details of Sortie: -
9/10 Cloud encountered and DR navigation to target, moderate flak, did a square search and then encountered intense and accurate flak, so presuming it to be Duisberg, bombed it.

Summary of Events: -
Weather - scattered squally showers, becoming fine, visibility 6-12 miles, deteriorating.

16 aircraft to stand by, five to lay mines in the Baltic, eight to bomb objective Duisberg and three to carry out intruder patrols in searchlight belts, to assist main effort.

1750 hrs - Gardeners cancelled.

Shadows of the Past 55

1800 hrs - All intruders took off and were successful in breaking up the searchlights. Of the eight bombers, none were able to bomb main objective. 1 aircraft did not take off owing to damage sustained in a taxiing accident. Flak estimated position of Duisberg, which was bombed by all aircraft and several burst seen through cloud, 10/10 cloud prevented any accurate bombing.

Results, BCWD: -
87 Aircraft - 47 Wellingtons, 26 Hampdens and 14 Whitleys, with eight further Hampdens carrying out searchlight suppression flights. The target was cloud-covered and only estimated positions were bombed. One Wellington lost.

AD896: Tony Pointer (W/Op/AG, far right) with his first crew. Dave Block (pilot), Brian Hugget (navigator), & Jock Cameron (W/Op/AG), July 25th, 1941.

Shadows of the Past
   Tenth Operation: Bombing Bremen, October 20th/21st, 1941

HAMPDEN AE132
P/O WOOD: pilot
Sgt WEST: navigator
Sgt GAUNT: wireless operator & air gunner
Sgt POINTER: air gunner
Up 1846 hrs, down 0152 hrs (7 hrs 5 mins)

Details of Sortie: -
No pinpoint obtained at Bremen except for searchlights. Circled round picking up rivers in light of numerous flares. Being unable to pinpoint - bombs dropped off DR position of Bremen. Flak exceptionally accurate.

Summary of Events: -
Weather fine at first, variable skies later and scattered squalls, wind 30 mph. 16 aircraft to stand by, six bombers and 10 fire-raisers to attack Bremen and two to lay mines in the area of the Fresian Islands.

1800 hrs - all aircraft took off at short intervals and two gardeners were successful in laying mines in the Fresian area. Owing to intense haze and darkness only five bombers successfully attacked the target, making pinpointing impossible. Two unsuccessful aircraft returned their bombs to base, but the others attacked DR position of target, Bremen town, Flak and searchlight concentrations in vicinity of target Oldenberg and Flarepath at Croningen. Several aircraft experienced severe icing and other difficulties included failure of intercom and heating systems and in only one case were bursts observed.

All 49 Squadron aircraft returned safely.

Results BCWD: -
153 Aircraft, consisting of 82 Hampdens, 48 Wellingtons, 15 Stirlings and eight Manchesters to two aiming points.

Five Aircraft lost - two Hampdens, two Wellingtons, and one Manchester. Returning crews claimed to have started fires in the target area. The Bremen report records only that this was a small raid and gave no details.

Sobering Thoughts

Results of Bombing November 10th/11th, 1941 - February 22nd, 1942

The two main factors in any military campaign are the results as compared with the cost of casualties sustained. Things were moving adversely against Bomber Command; it is thought that heavy casualties can be sustained as long as operable results are being achieved. Bomber Command throughout this period, however, was definitely not getting the results it would have liked and the losses in men and machines were unjustified. The evidence available on bombing results makes for sobering thoughts. Firstly, the disturbing reports of the ineffectiveness of attacks on targets in Germany; these reports coming through neutral countries for many months. In the first six months of 1941, the RAF collected its own evidence from three sources. Firstly, there were many verbal reports from the returning bomber crews, these were processed and passed on with a certain amount of optimism by squadrons and groups, to finally arrive on a report on which most public announcements were made. Secondly, there was the photographic reconnaissance unit, formed to obtain evidence of damage carried out to enemy installations; only a minimum amount of good photos could be used and these sometimes conflicted sharply with the crew reports and was not always accepted as conclusive. Thirdly, the only real evidence held by the RAF was the accumulated stock of individual aircraft bombing photographs taken by that proportion of the forces whose planes were fitted with bombing cameras. It was in August 1942 the Butt Report was completed – its conclusions were illuminating.

Butt analysed 4,065 individual aircraft photographs taken during 100 night raids in June and July 1941. Despite the fact that it was usually the more experienced crews in the squadron who were given these cameras, only one in four of the crews which claimed to have bombed a target in Germany were found to have been within five miles of that target. In the full moon period, the proportion of crews whose bombs fell in the five mile zone increased to two in five on all targets (about one in three over German targets), while in the none moon periods of each month, the five mile zone was hit by one in fifteen crews on all targets (about one in

Shadows of the Past

twenty on German targets). In the areas affected by industrial haze, the proportion of successful crews was considerably less. These poor and very disappointing figures were to be compounded by the fact that only the photos of crews reporting successful bombing in the first instance had contributed to the figures. A third of all crews despatched on operations did not even claim to have reached the target area.

Very early on in the war, it became apparent that daylight raids brought high losses, bombers could not defend themselves and flight cover was not an option over Germany. Later in 1944-45 with the use of drop tanks, allied forces gave cover virtually all the way to the target and back. The North American P-51 Mustang, with its Rolls-Royce Merlin engine built under license in America, was to be many a bomber crews' saviour. Night time raids were to be preferred by the British bomber squadrons. During this early period of the war, bomber crews were not in the picture regarding the overall situation. Some had good results, some had bad and as far as losses were concerned, it was that other part of 'the equation' – that it happened to other aircrew.

Operations July $7^{th}/8th$ to November 10th had cost 414 night bombers and 112 day bombers lost over enemy territory, in the sea or shot down over England by German intruders. These losses were approximately identical to the numbers of the entire front line strength of aircraft and crews in four months. The percentage loss of aircraft despatched was 3.5% by night and 7.1% by day.

Eleventh Operation – Anti-Shipping & Mine Laying in Kiel Bay
November $1^{st}/2^{nd}$, 1941

HAMPDEN AE132
P/O WOOD: pilot
Sgt WEST: navigator
Sgt POINTER: wireless operator
Sgt GAUNT: 2nd wireless operator
Up 1951hrs, down 0358 hrs (7 hrs 7 mins)

Shadows of the Past

Details of Sortie: -
Vegetable planted in primary position from 700 feet. Light very good 8/10ths cloud at 2000 feet. Fix on coast at Bult and timed run to position. Parachute seen to open and splash seen. Wing bombs returned.

Summary of Events: -
Four aircraft to standby for antishipping mine laying in Kiel Bay, two aircraft successfully laid mines, the other two aircraft sought shipping targets in the Frisians. In heavy rain with poor visibility 1,500 yards, Flight Lieutenant de Mestre (AD980) and crew attacked shipping from 1,000 feet. A near miss was made on one ship, but the remainder overshot. During the attack the Hampden was hit by flak and the rear gunner Pilot Officer Holmes was wounded. The crew returned to Scampton safely. The second aircraft detailed for anti shipping was piloted by Squadron Leader Drakes (AE224). Nothing was heard from this crew after take off. It is thought that a night-fighter shot them down over the North Sea.

Squadron Leader David Baron Drakes and crew are remembered on the Runnymede Memorial.

FTR AE224
S/L   D B DRAKES: pilot   (missing)
P/O W H CHEETHAM: air gunner & observer (missing)
P/O V D BEANEY: navigator   (missing)
F/Sgt W A WATSON: (missing)

Aircraft & Crew Losses

Essen Intruder, November 8th/9th, 1941

Three aircraft were despatched to Essen. One of these was to bomb and was piloted by Sergeant Freeman and his crew. Freeman, a little later was to become Tubby's pilot (64125). This aircraft was followed by two intruders, one of these P1206 (EA-Z) piloted by Warrant Officer Christopher Saunders DFM and crew were shot down by a German night fighter flown by *Oberfeldwebel* Wey of 11/NJG2. The aircraft was hit over the Dutch coast and set on fire. It was seen to circle before crashing

Shadows of the Past

at Berkhout, South West of Hoorn in Holland. The wreckage sank deep into the marshy ground and the bodies of Sergeants John Kehoe (of Eire) and Stanley Mullenger have never been recovered. The pilot, Warrant Officer C A Saunders, and navigator, Sergeant James D'arcy, are both buried in Bergen general cemetery.

FTR P1206
W/O C A SAUNDERS: pilot   (killed)
Sgt J M D'ARCY: navigator   (killed)
Sgt J E KEHOC: wireless operator & air gunner   (missing)
Sgt S G MULLENGER: as above   (missing)

Flying Accident, including the Hackthorn Hall Tragedy, November 11th, 1941

In the late afternoon of Tuesday, November 11th, 1941, Sergeant Pilot Keith Bryant was detailed to ferry X3135 over to Dunholme Lodge. The pilot took along two members of the ground crew, LAC Andrew Wilson and AC2 Walter Fulcher. The Hampden was seen to make a steep left hand turn before crashing into the ground at Hackthorn Hall, north east of Scampton Aerodrome. Tragically, all on board were killed.

Crashed X3135
Sgt K BRYANT: pilot   (killed)
LAC A G WILSON: (killed)
AC2 W H FULCHER: (killed)

November 25th, 1941

Just two weeks after the Hackthorn Hall tragedy, another of the Squadron's Hampdens crashed whilst on a training flight. 20 year old Sergeant Pilot Ron Hough and Sergeant George Edward Smith were both killed instantly when their aircraft AD759 spun into the ground at Scamlesby, on the Lincolnshire Wolds. During low flying at 1455 hrs on the afternoon of Tuesday, November 25th, Hampden AD759 was seen making a very low approach towards the village of Scamlesby where Sergeant Smith's family lived. Tragically, the Hampden's wing struck

Shadows of the Past

the ground and the aircraft crashed through the fields just on the edge of the village. Smith, whose relatives still live in the village, is buried in St Martin's churchyard, Scamlesby, whilst Hough rests in Clayton-Le-Moor's cemetery in Lancashire.

Crashed AD759
Sgt R R HUGH: pilot   (killed)
Sgt G E SMITH: wireless operator & air gunner   (killed)

Twelfth Operation: – Bombing Lorient Docks, France
November 23rd/24th, 1941

HAMPDEN AD896
Sgt JENKINS: pilot
Sgt CLOUGH: navigator
Sgt WOODREFFE: wireless operator & air gunner
Sgt GAUNT: air gunner
Up 1614 hrs, down 2215 hrs (6 hrs 1 min)

Details of Sortie: -
Very little cloud and good visibility. Target seen in moonlight. Bombs went alongside railway lines, burst seen, no fires and no opposition from heavy flak on coast, which had fired on outward journey.

Summary of Events: -
Weather fog - violent squally showers, with hail, low cloud and poor visibility.

18 aircraft to stand by to bomb the docks at Lorient. All aircraft took off and 13 were successful in attacking primary target in conditions of slight cloud and good visibility. Of the aircraft which were unsuccessful, two were unable to locate the target owing to being off track and returned with their bombs. Another could not positively pinpoint the docks and jettisoned wing bombs to gain height. One aircraft suffered complete W/T failure. Five aircraft reported fires seen and in three cases, bursts were observed.

All aircraft returned safely from this operation.

Results, BCWD: -
51 Hampdens and 2 Manchesters attacked, large fires seen in vicinity of docks, there were no losses.

Aircraft & Crew Losses

December 8th, 1941: Killed on Active Service

The Squadron suffered its sixth flying accident casualty within a month, when Sergeant Thomas Hardisty was reported killed on active service. On Monday, December 8th, Hardisty was the Wireless Operator on Hampden AE227 taking part in a practice flight around the local area of Scampton. For some unexplained reason, Sergeant Hardisty fell to his death from the aircraft. The Welton police reported that an airman, subsequently identified as Thomas Hardisty, had been killed after baling out over Sudbrooke, there is no further information as to the cause of this tragedy. 21 year old Sergeant Thomas Hardisty is buried in St John the Baptist churchyard at Scampton.

December 12th, 1941 – Bombing Bremerhaven in Daylight

The unit despatched two aircraft to attack the barracks at Bremerhaven. The Hodges crew (AT124) of Cadman, Fry and Ellis were unable to attack the barracks due to lack of cloud cover over the Frisian Islands and the crew returned safely with its bomb load.

The Robinson crew (AD979) consisting of Black, Price and Mossop could not locate their target (barracks) at Cuxhaven and went on to bomb and strafe the local aerodrome.

Facing intense ground fire, Sergeant Pilot Robinson took his aircraft down to l00 feet. to carry out the attack and during the assault, one hanger was seen to blow up and two aircraft were set on fire on the ground, also the town was machine gunned. Inevitably, the Hampden sustained numerous flak hits and was severely shot up. Sadly, Flight Sergeant Stuart Black RNZAF was struck by fragments from a cannon shell and killed. The

Shadows of the Past 63

pilot now had to get the battered aircraft back to England, making landfall over the Norfolk coast, the aircraft made for Bircham Newton, where without the use of Hydraulics, the pilot managed a successful crash-landing timed at 1635 hrs. Flight Sergeant Black is buried in Great Bircham churchyard in Norfolk.

Crashed AD979
Sgt R J ROBINSON: pilot   (unhurt)
F/Sgt S C BLACK (RNZAF): pilot & navigator   (killed)
Sgt J PRICE: wireless operator & air gunner (unhurt)
Sgt W MOSSOP: as above,   (unhurt)

Thirteenth Operation: Bombing Huls (Camara) December 28th/29th, 1941

HAMPDEN AE12
Sgt HAMER: pilot
Sgt HADDOCK: navigator
Sgt MINCAIN: wireless operator
Sgt GAUNT: air gunner
Up 1735 hrs, down 0014 hrs (6 hrs 39 mins)

Sgt Hamer (pilot).

Huls synthetic oil plant, photographed from Tubby's aircraft: direct hits, December 28th, 1941.

Shadows of the Past

Details of Sortie: -
Target - synthetic rubber works at Huls.

No cloud and good visibility. Pinpointed railway, river and canal. Bombs released on target when in sight and one burst and large fire seen visible 60 miles after leaving. Flak very accurate. Nickels over Wesel on return.

Summary of Events: -
Weather isolated snow showers and later fog. Good visibility decreasing heavy frost.

20 aircraft to standby for bombing attack on Synthetics Rubber works at Huls, alternative town of Munster and any resort in built-up areas NW Germany. All aircraft took off at intervals and 17 found and successfully bombed main objective, in excellent visibility. Owing to intense AA barrage, one aircraft had to bomb Dortmund Dock area and being unable to locate Huls, another attacked a factory in Essen. One aircraft was missing from operations; no signals were received from it. Of the successful aircraft, 14 saw bursts or large fires resulting from their attacks and several huge explosions resulted. Excellent photographs were taken in several cases, showing the target to be hit directly many times.

Missing Aircraft: -

Ftr. AE419 piloted by Sergeant Archie Watt and crew. The bodies of this crew have never been recovered. It is believed that the aircraft came down in the sea. Sergeant Watt and his crew are remembered on the Runnymede Memorial. It was a very sad note on which to finish the troubled year of 1941.

FIR AE419
Sgt A C WATT: pilot   (missing)
Sgt E G SAWDY: navigator & pilot   (missing)
F/Sgt E C ATKINSON: wireless operator & air gunner   (missing)
Sgt H W WISDOM: wireless operator   (missing)

All the above are missing in action.

BCWD: -
Total effort for the night 217 sorties, 4 aircraft lost.

Results: -
Excellent bombing backed by photographs. 81 Hampdens in all attacked. Four aircraft lost in total.

Aircraft & Crew Losses

January 6th, 1942 – Crash at South Carlton

0700 hrs on the morning of Tuesday, January 6th, Hampden AD896 'M-mother' approached Scampton to land after a night of training. As the aircraft passed over the small hamlet of South Carlton, one of the engines suddenly cut out. The aircraft stalled, then fell into Middle Street, killing two of the crew, including the pilot, Sergeant Godfrey West. Also killed in this tragic accident was wireless operator Sergeant George Atkins. Fortunately, there were no civilian casualties in the Hamlet. It cannot be established if these were the only two airmen aboard this aircraft that fatal morning.

Crashed AD896
Sgt G L WEST: pilot   (killed)
Sgt G T ATKINS: wireless operator & air gunner   (killed)

January 9th/10th, 1942: Bombing & Mining in Brest

14 aircraft sent to Brest, nine aircraft to bomb the battle cruisers in Brest harbour and five to plant mines in the Brest area. Of the minelayers, three were successful in planting their mines and one was unable to find the target area. Sadly, the fifth was reported missing. Pilot Officer Thomas Jacobs (AD909) and crew are presumed to have come down into the sea and their bodies have never been recovered. The crew is remembered on the Runnymede Memorial.

FTR AD909
P/O T F JACOBS: pilot   (missing)

P/O P T CLOSE: air observer   (missing)
Sgt W B ROBERTSON: wireless operator & air gunner   (missing)
Sgt J WARREN: as above   (missing)

Aircraft & Crew Losses

January 21st/22nd, 1942 – Bombing Emden.

The Squadron sent five Hampdens to attack Emden. Two aircraft failed to attack any target owing to icing and failure of heating and two aircraft bombed the primary target. No signals were received from the fifth aircraft and it was reported missing.

Flying Officer Alex Harvey (AT148) and crew were shot down over Groningen by *Oberfeldwebel* Paul Gildner of 11/NJG.2. Sadly, all the crew perished when S-Sugar fell to earth near the farm of Mr Ritsema at Roodehaan, Noorddijk, in Holland.

The crew rest together in Noorddijk general cemetery.

FTR AT148
F/O A M HARVEY: pilot   (killed)
Sgt W A GREY: navigator   (killed)
Sgt J W HALLAM: wireless operator & air gunner   (killed)
Sgt R M KNAPMAN: air gunner   (killed)

January 25th/26th, 1942 – Bombing battle cruisers.

The Squadron despatched 17 Hampdens on a cold night with snow and ice on the ground. At 1712 hours, immediately after take-off, Hampden O-Orange, piloted by Sergeant Charles Stewart (AT129), crashed to earth near the small hamlet of Bransby, between Sturton and Saxilby - there were no survivors. It is thought that the aircraft may have been brought down by ice collecting on its flying surfaces.

Crashed AT129
Sgt C D S STEWART: pilot   (killed)

Sgt A HIBBIT:	wireless operator & air gunner	(killed)
Sgt K E NORTHROP:	as above	(killed)
Sgt L A JARDINE:	as above	(killed)

Of the aircraft that continued on towards Brest, one returned to base with mechanical problems, 8 failed to attack any target owing to the effect of 10/10 cloud making fixes impossible. The remainder attacked alternative targets within the dock area. There were no further losses.

Fourteenth Operation: Bombing Battlecrusiers at Brest
Scharnhort & Prinz Eugen, January 27th/28th, 1942

HAMPDEN AE112
Sgt FREEMAN: pilot
Sgt BUSH: navigator
Sgt GAUNT: wireless operator & air gunner
Sgt OSBALDESTON: air gunner
Up 0017 hrs, down 0628 hrs (6 hrs 45 mins)

Details of Sortie: -
Primary target bombed from 12,500 feet on 060Ú in good noon light and fair conditions. Smoke screen and landmarks assisted identification of Cap St. Mathieu and Rescanvel Premontery. Docks in sight on release, one burst seen.

Summary of Events: -
Weather slight snow, ground frost, otherwise clear and bright with cloud patches.

17 aircraft detailed to attack battlecruisers *Scharnhorst* and *Prince Eugen* at Brest harbour. All aircraft took off at short intervals and six aircraft were successful in attacking the primary objective. Of these, four saw bursts, but no results, although all aircraft had the targets in their sights on releasing bombs. Three aircraft attacked alternative targets, dock installations in the area. Haze prevented positive identification of target in these cases – no bursts were seen here. Flak was intense and accurate. Seven aircraft failed to attack any target owing to heating failures and in four cases, inability to find target and navigational errors. No losses.

Shadows of the Past 68

Results, BSWD: -
All aircraft returned safely to Scampton.

Brest Harbour was possibly the most protected target area in Europe, completely surrounded by every calibre of anti aircraft gun. Also smoke screens were used extensively.

Sgt Ken Bush, killed in 1944.

Tubby, 1941.

Sgt Terry Freeman (Tubby's pilot) 1942.

Fifteenth Operation: Bombing Battlecrusiers at Brest
Scharnhorst & Gnisenau
Light crusiser Prinz Eugen, *January 31st, 1942*

HAMPDEN AE132
Sgt FREEMAN: pilot
Sgt KIRBY: navigator
Sgt GAUNT: wireless operator & air gunner
Sgt OSBALDESTON: air gunner
Up 1710 hrs, down 2320 hrs (6 hrs 10 mins)

Details of Sortie: -
Alternative (Docks) bombed at 12,000 feet in 8-10 cloud. Owing to Under weather conditions battleship could not be seen. Bombs seen to enter dock area, but no burst seen. Two bundles of nickels in target area.

Shadows of the Past

Summary of Events: -
Weather snow at intervals, increasing later vis. 2-5 miles, wind S.E. but variable.

18 aircraft to stand by to bomb battlecruisers at Brest. Alternatively the dock area. All aircraft took off at short intervals and eight aircraft failed to attack any target, this was due to two cases of engine failure, one of oxygen failure and the rest on account of inability to see the target because of the smoke screen. One of these aircraft jettisoned bombs which were fused near D'oussant and in three cases Nickels were dropped from the remainder of the aircraft. One bombed the primary target and the remainder attacked the docks, six aircraft observing bursts in the area.

Superb (and highly unofficial!) study of Tubby, Ken & Terry on Hampden AE132.

49 Sqn & Hampden, 1941, Tubby 3rd from right, back row.

All aircraft found the smoke screen over the docks interfered with proper identification and observation of results.

This raid was perhaps one of the last raids carried out by the RAF before the German Battle Squadron moved up the channel towards their home ports. The defences around Brest were being stepped up and as a result, three Manchesters and two Hampdens were reported missing. All 49 squadron returned home.

Results, BCWD: -
Of the 72 aircraft that attacked Brest, three Manchesters and two Hampdens were lost. The Manchesters were from 61 squadron, which had sent only nine aircraft on the raid.

The Scharnhorst & Gneisenau

These two mighty battlecruisers, the pride of the German navy, were both completed 1938-9 with a displacement full load of 38,900 tons.

A length of 234.9 mtrs with a beam of 30.0 mtrs and design draft of 817 mtrs was formidable indeed. Carrying a complement of 1,670 men, the armament consisted of nine 11 inch guns (3 x 3), twelve 5.9 inch (6 x 2),

14 4.1 inch guns (7 x 2), 16 37mm guns (8 x 2), six 21 inch torpedo tubes and LX aircraft. The ships belt armour up to 13.8 inches thick and turrets up to 14.2 inches.

These ocean raiders had many successful engagements. The main purpose of these surface raiders was to sink allied convoys without engaging the accompanying battleships; hit and run without sustaining any damage.

On June 8th, 1940, the raiders found the aircraft carrier *HMS Glorious* with little protection, a few destroyers and no aircraft in the air, they quietly dispatched the carrier to the depths using gun fire - this was a huge loss to the admiralty and the accompanying destroyers as well, but not before *HMS Acasto* torpedoed the *Scharnhorst*, putting her in dock for five months. Breaking out again with some difficulty, the pair on March 15th/16th, 1941, intercepted an unprotected convoy and proceeded to sink sixteen merchant ships.

The invasion of Norway saw the *Gneisenau* covering the landings, the British battle cruiser *HMS Renown* engaged and put 3 - 15 inch shells into her, Admiral Lutjens broke off the engagement and fled among the frequent snow squalls.

Shadows of the Past

The pair were not together again until January 1941. They arrived at Brest on March 22nd, 1941, for a period of three months, to complete the necessary refitting. The RAF raids kept the ships there for 11 months until the breakout on February 11th, 1942.

Operation Cerberus

The Channel dash by the Scharnhorst, Gneisenau, Prince Eugen *and accompanying ships 2300 hours, February 11th, 1942*

This powerful squadron, under Vice-Admiral Ciliax, slipped their moorings at Brest, moved out and rounded Ushant, following a narrow channel previously swept of mines and marked at various viewpoints by small anchored patrol craft moving in an eastward direction, up through the English Channel. A catalogue of errors enabled the squadron to move unopposed, right up and through Capgriz Nez.

Various attempts were made to attack the Squadron, but with little or no success and sustaining high losses. Six Fleet Air Arm Fairey Swordfish aircraft from Manston were shot down in one raid. Bristol Beauforts from their Cornwall base also took heavy losses, scoring no hits on the battleships. The early gardening operations were to have some success for the RAF: the *Gneisenau* and *Scharnhorst*, moving eastward of the Dutch island of Terschelling, hit mines; the *Scharnhorst* was seriously damaged and struggled to Wilhemshaven on one engine, while being seriously flooded by an estimated 1,000 tons of water. The other ships reached comparative safety of various Elbe ports.

The earlier mine-laying operations by No 5 Group were concentrated in an area to the North and West of Terschelling, where the *Scharnhorst* struck one mine at 1430 hrs, off Flushing, and another at 2134 hrs north of Terschelling. So we can, with some justification, acredit this success to No.5 Group's earlier efforts.

The movement of the capital ships brought to an end perhaps the largest combined effort of the RAF against naval power, a task that would not be missed. During the period the ships were at Brest and La Pallice. The

Shadows of the Past

RAF despatched 3,599 aircraft sorties, 2,692 aircraft had attacked with the loss of 53 machines, 4,118 tons of bombs had been dropped on the two docks and ships.

These capital ships at anchor would never again be ocean raiders. The *Scharnhorst* was sunk by British warships after a classic gunnery duel; early in the engagement the *Scharnhorst* suffered a direct hit on her radar scanner. The engagement that night rendered her blind, the British war ships stood off and shelled her at will. Loss of life was to be enormous, many sailors were drowned, help was not on hand and fearing U-boat attacks, the British ships could not stop and pick up survivors.

The German warships lying at anchor, Brest, July 21st, 1941. Photo by George Webb.

Scharnhorst's sister ship *Gneisenau* was bombed whilst in harbour at Kiel, with her forward end virtually blown off, she was never re-commissioned and was dismantled in 1943. The attack was carried out by 49 Squadron and other Wellington and Halifax squadrons. Both 49 Squadron Hampdens involved reported hits on the Gneisenau.

Aircraft & Crew Losses

February 11th, 1942 – The 'Channel Dash'

In recent months, Bomber Command had dropped over 3,000 tons of bombs on the battle cruisers *Schaarnhorst* and *Gneisanau* and the light

Shadows of the Past

cruiser *Prince Eugen*, as they resided in the French port of Brest. The two larger ships had both been badly damaged and the threat of further damage had prevented the ships from sailing out into the Atlantic on another raid against allied shipping.

As previously stated, in a daring and well executed operation, the Germans sailed their three battle cruisers with accompanying destroyers and minelayers straight through the English Channel in the most appalling weather, as cover to the protection of the German ports. What followed on behalf of the British Command has been labelled a catalogue of catastrophes. The capital ships arrived at their destinations, but not before striking mines dropped by 5 Group and 49 Squadron in particular. The *Scharnhorst* hit two mines and the *Gneisenau* one. Most of Bomber Command was stood down for the day, only 5 Group was at four hours notice. The bomber squadrons made a frantic effort to prepare planes for attacks which were mounted in three waves. Other aircraft of Coastal and Fighter Commands and of the Fleet Air Arm were also involved.

49 Squadron's participation was prompted by a signal from Group received at 1000 hours, requesting 20 aircraft to attack the *Scharnhorst* and *Gneisenau* at sea. Sergeant Hamer AD968, Flying Officer Jenkins P1153 and Flight Sergeant Pollitt AE132, three of Tubby's previous pilots, were on this bombing mission. During the operation, Flying Officer Jenkins' P1153 and crew reported being attacked by a Wellington bomber off The Hague – the offending aircraft had no squadron markings!
In low cloud and rain, with extremely poor visibility, only three of the Squadron's aircraft found the primary target and dropped their bombs, but with no hits on the targets. The Squadron lost four aircraft and crews; it is now believed that two of those aircraft were shot down by German fighters, AE132 piloted by Flight Sergeant Charles Pollitt and AE396 flown by Sergeant Edward Phillips, both of which were enveloped by the cold North Sea.

The other two aircraft, AE249, piloted by Sergeant Mervyn Halt, and P5324, flown by Sergeant Thomas Downs, also came down in the sea, though the cause cannot be determined. The tragic loss of these brave young airmen was compounded by the fact that little damage had been

Shadows of the Past

done to the large German flotilla. At Scampton the following day, life went on as usual, no 'ops' were ordered, which gave ground crews a chance to catch up on their work.

The Channel Dash & 49 Squadron's Involvement, February 12th, 1942

The heavily armed battle cruisers and their accompanying flotilla would exact a heavy toll on the attacking aircraft. Fighter command lost 16 aircraft and the Fleet Air Arm six Swordfish destroyed. Bomber Command's contribution to the action involved 244 aircraft, of which 15 were lost in action and a further two crashing on return. 5 Group had been on a four hour 'standby', as other bomber squadrons made frantic efforts to prepare their aircraft. Later in the day, 5 Group were to contribute 64 Hampdens and 15 Manchesters to attack the German warships. In all, nine Hampdens were reported missing and one crashed on return.

In low cloud and rain, with poor visibility, only three of the aircraft found their primary targets. All three attacked, but no hits were observed. Four of 49 Squadron aircraft did not return and all their crews were lost.

Tubby had flown many times with Flight Sergeant Pollitt; he would be sadly missed.

49 Squadron's Aircraft & Crew Losses in the Channel Dash.

FTR P5324
Sgt DOWNES:	pilot	(killed)
Sgt D G F POXON:	air gunner	(killed)
Sgt B HUNTER:	wireless operator & air gunner	(killed)
Sgt T H F WOOD:	pilot	(missing)

FTR AE132
Sgt F S POLLITT:	pilot	(missing)
Sgt R J CRIDGE:	wireless operator	(missing)
Sgt I S GREENSTREET:	air observer	(missing)
Sgt W SMITH:	air gunner	(missing)

Shadows of the Past

FTR AE396
Sgt E W PHILLIPS:	pilot	(missing)
Sgt A JACKSON:	wireless operator	(missing)
Sgt K W HEARD:	pilot	(missing)
Sgt L C TOGHILL:	air gunner	(missing)

FTR AE240
Sgt M H HOLT:	pilot	(missing)
Sgt S W A WAY:	wireless operator & air gunner	(missing)
Sgt E G GREEN:	pilot	(missing)
Sgt C L LEE:	air observer	(missing)

Aircraft & Crew Losses

February 14th/15th, 1942 – Bombing Mannheim

The Squadron had 12 aircraft airborne, around 1600 hrs, bound for the railway station at Manheim. In all, 98 aircraft attacked the target, which received only slight damage. Two aircraft from 49 Squadron were lost, though the two crews survived.

F/Sgt Pollitt, Tubby's pilot on the Cherbourg raid, missing on February 12th, 1942, Channel raid.

Pilot Officer Ralph Allsebrook and crew ditched within sight of the English coast: a Bristol Beaufighter returning from patrol spotted the lights in the sea. A naval coastguard launch went out and rescued the frost-bitten crew. Ralph Allsebrook went on to fly Lancasters with 49 Squadron, eventually transferring to 617, where on September 15th/16th, 1943, his crew were shot down and killed whilst attacking the Dortmund EMS canal.

Sergeant Hamer and crew managed to reach England after nine hrs flying. Short on fuel, the pilot made a forced landing. M-Mother came to earth at Glossmore Farm on Ponders Bridge, despite the heavy landing in which the Hampden was destroyed, all the crew escaped.

Shadows of the Past

FTR (ditched)
P/O R A P ALLESBROOK: pilot   (rescued)
Sgt STANBRIDGE: air observer   (rescued)
Sgt WILKINSON: wireless operator & air gunner (rescued)
Sgt WOOLGAR: as above   (rescued)

Crashed AT1I2
Sgt R N HAMER: pilot   (unhurt)
Sgt HADDOCK: (unhurt)
Sgt MINCHIN: (unhurt)
Sgt WATCHORN: (unhurt)

February 16th/17th, 1942: Minelaying & Nickels (leaflets)

49 Squadron carried out their duties with mixed success. One aircraft failed to return. It is presumed that Flying Officer Jenkins (AT124) and crew came down in the North Sea. The bodies of this unfortunate crew have never been recovered - they are remembered on the Runnymede Memorial.

FTR AT124
F/O G R JENKINS: pilot   (missing)
P/O J T B CLOUGH: navigator   (missing)
Sgt J A STEELE: wireless operator & air gunner   (missing)
Sgt J A WOODRUFFE: as above   (missing)

Tubby flew as W/AG with Gordon Jenkins and crew on the Lorient raid November 23rd, 1941.

Sixteenth Operation: Mining Heliogland, February 24th/25th, 1942

HAMPDEN AE368
Sgt FREEMAN: pilot
Sgt BUSH: navigator
Sgt GAUNT: wireless operator & air gunner
Sgt OSBALDESTON: air gunner
Up 1802 hrs, down 2315 hrs (5 hrs 13 mins)

Shadows of the Past

Details of Sortie: -
Last resort selected – Nordeney – and mine laid at 700 feet. Cloud base below 500 feet and no results seen.

Summary of Events: -
Weather: north wind five –ten mph, slight snow, generally overcast, but visibility three - six miles and improving.

15 aircraft to stand by, of which 14 to lay mines off Heligoland Bight and one to mine off Terschelling.

All aircraft took off at intervals and owing to cloud, haze and ice in the sea, seven aircraft laid mines in last resort targets, a position five-eight miles off Frisians, Nordeney, Schiermonnikoog, Ameland and Texel. Five aircraft mined in primary position and three failed to lay vegetables at all, but returned them owing to impossibility of pinpointing any target due to cloud. In seven cases, the mines were seen to enter the water in selected positions.

BCWD: -
42 Hampdens and nine Manchesters minelaying in the Frisians and off Wilhelmshaven and Heligoland. Two Hampdens lost, five aircraft on leaflet flights to France and Belgium without loss.

Two Hampdens were from 144 Squadron.
Seventeenth Operation: Mining Heligoland, February 26th/27th, 1942

HAMPDEN AE368
Sgt FREEMAN: pilot
Sgt BUSH: navigator
Sgt GAUNT: wireless operator & air gunner
Sgt OSBALDESTON: air gunner
Up 1800 hrs, down 2315 hrs (5 hrs 15 mins)

Details of Sortie: -
Vegetables returned to base owing to inability to pinpoint owing to ice around the coastline.

Summary of Events: -
Weather – NE wind five-ten mph, cloud with occasional snow, 8/10 cloud, surface icing.

Eight aircraft detailed to lay mines off Heligoland approach and four to bomb German cruisers in floating dock at Kiel.

All aircraft took off at short intervals with six mining aircraft successfully finding primary mining area and leaving mines. Seeing them enter the water. Of the two aircraft of this class which were unsuccessful, one returned owing to engine failure and the other owing to inability to pinpoint. Ice around the coastline was making it very difficult for the bombers. Two aircraft were successful in attacking the main objective and one of these saw fire results from the bursts (almost successful sortie). The other two aircraft returned their loads to base, as unable to climb through cloud on account of severe icing. Apart from icing conditions, generally weather conditions were better than usual this month, visibility being 20 miles or more.

BCWD: -
A total of 49 aircraft - 33 Wellingtons, 10 Hampdens and six Halifaxes to attack the floating dock at Kiel. Two Wellingtons and one Halifax lost. It was a night of mixed fortunes; crews claimed good results in weather with bombs close to the floating dock. A high explosive bomb scored a direct hit on the bows of the *Gueisenau*, causing severe damage and killing 116 men in her crew. This proved to be the end of the Gueisenau as a fighting unit. Her guns were later removed for coastal defence work and she was taken to Gydnia but never repaired. Bombing in the town of Kiel destroyed many houses and killed 16 people. A report from Denmark shows how some of the bomber crews failed to locate Kiel accurately and dropped their loads on towns on the islands and coast of east Denmark. Damage and casualties were caused in Vejle (three killed, six injured) and Odense (one killed and seven injured). Vejle was 100 miles north of Kiel.

Minor operations, 27 Hampdens mine laying off German ports - five Hampdens on leaflet flights - no losses.

Shadows of the Past
Eighteenth Operation: Bombing Essen, March 8th, 1942

HAMPDEN AE241
Sgt FREEMAN: pilot
Sgt BUSH: navigator
Sgt GAUNT: wireless operator & air gunner
Sgt LOGIE: air gunner
Up 0022 hrs, down 0630 hrs (6 hrs 8 mins)

Details of Sortie: -
Attacked town from 12,000 feet, visibility being 8-10 miles. Map read, with flares, to target and bombs seen in area, with three ensuing bursts, nine fires seen. Nickels over Essen.

Summary of Events: -
Weather overcast, visibility good, freezing level surface, winds light easterly.

14 aircraft detailed to attack old town of Essen. One aircraft was cancelled, one suffered undercarriage collapse prior to takeoff, but the remainder took off and 10 successfully attacked primary objective in conditions of good light and eight saw bursts and fires result from attack. These were in the target area. One pilot bombed alternative objective, Dortmund, and saw burst result. One aircraft returned with bomb load owing to intercommunication failure, landing at Waddington. One W/T failure occurred, but did not prevent aircraft from proceeding. Heavy Flak, slight damage two aircraft and one case of oxygen failure occurred.

On a clear night and despite the leading aircraft being fitted with 'GEE', the 211 bombers were prevented from making accurate attacks due to industrial green haze. Eight aircraft failed to return, but all 49 Squadron returned safely.

Results: -
This was yet another major step forward, a heavy raid on the previously difficult target of Essen, with leading aircraft now fitted with GEE (Navigational aid). Eight aircraft lost – five Wellingtons, two Manchesters and one Stirling.

Shadows of the Past

Industrial haze over Essen prevented accurate bombing and the raid was a big disappointment. GEE enables the aircrafts to reach approximate area of the target. Photographic evidence showed that the main target, the Krupps factory, was not hit, but some bombs fell in the southern part of Essen. Essen reports only a light raid, with a few houses and a church destroyed. Ten people reported killed and 19 missing. The most noticeable incident was the burning down of a well-known restaurant, the *Blumenhof*, in the Grugo Park, which was being used to house foreign workers.

Nineteenth Operation: Bombing Essen, March 10$^{th/11th}$, 1942

HAMPDEN AE241
Sgt FREEMAN: pilot
Sgt BUSH: navigator
Sgt OSBALDESTON: air gunner
Sgt GAUNT: wireless operator & air gunner
Up 1915 hrs, down 0330 hrs (6 hrs 15 mins)

Details of Sortie: -
Unable to locate primary target, bombed concentration on fires on ETA alternative target, burst observed. One 500 lb GP bomb hung up, six bundles nickels dropped over target area. Crash landed Manston.

No reference was made about what happened to the bomb hung up.

Tubby's logbook records (S.O.S fixes Heston) pranged Margate (cracked ribs – Margate General Hospital), it would be some weeks before Tubby would be fit for duty.

Summary of Events: -
Weather mainly fair – local mist patches, wind light SW mild.

11 aircraft took off, five only attacked alternative target, fires seen at Essen as a result. One aircraft returned owing to failure of intercommunication, one aircraft returned due to failure of oil system, one aircraft due to failure of undercarriage not retracting, one aircraft failed to return. One returning crash-landed at Manston due to fuel

Shadows of the Past

shortage, the W/Op AG, Sergeant Gaunt, being slightly injured. One aircraft returned owing to sickness of pilot after approximately 45 minutes flying. All aircraft dropped nickels; one sustained numerous shrapnel holes as a result of heavy flak.

Four aircraft failed to return from the raid and one of these came from 49 Squadron. Pilot Officer Bill Andrews, AT174 and crew were sadly all killed when brought down over Germany. The crew is buried alongside each other in the Reichwald Forest war cemetery near Kleve.

FTR AT174
P/O WHT ANDREWS: pilot   (killed)
Sgt ST DREW: wireless operator & air gunner   (killed)
P/O JB DUNNE: air observer   (killed)
Sgt AA BOURNE: wireless operator & air gunner   (killed)

BCWD: March 10th/11th, 1942 (Results of first Lancaster raid):-
126 Aircraft - 56 Wellingtons, 43 Hampdens, 13 Manchesters, 12 Stirlings, two Lancasters. This was the first participation of Lancasters in a raid on a German target. Four aircraft, two Hampdens, one Stirling and one Wellington lost. This was another disappointing raid with unexpected cloud being the main cause of poor bombing. 62 crews claimed to have bombed Essen. 35 crews bombed alternative targets. The report from Essen shows that only two bombs fell on industrial targets and railway lines near the Krupps factory, also one house destroyed and two damaged in residential areas. Five Germans were killed by a flak shell, which descended and exploded on the ground.

Aircraft & Crew Losses

March 10th/11th, 1942: Bombing Essen.

The Squadron contributed 11 Hampdens to attack on point 'B' the old town of Essen. It proved to be an evening of mixed fortunes. Having various problems, four aircraft returned to Scampton. Sgt Freeman (AE241) made a forced landing in a field at Spratling Street, Near Manston, Sergeant Gaunt the Wireless Operator/Air Gunner was slightly hurt and spent a couple of weeks in Margate General Hospital. Sadly

Shadows of the Past

Pilot Officer Bill Andrews (AT174) and crew were killed when E-Eco was brought down over Germany. The crew are buried alongside each other in the Reichswald Forest War Cemetery, near Kleve.

FTP AT174
P/O W H T ANDREWS: pilot   (killed)
Sgt S T DREW: wireless operator & air gunner   (killed)
P/O J B DUNNE: air observer   (killed)
Sgt A A GOULD: wireless operator & air gunner   (killed)

March 17th, 1942

Tragedy again: Pilot Officers Derek Cook and Bob Manders were both killed when their Hampden flew into a hill in fog. The accident happened 1125 hrs at Derry Farm, near Branscombe in Devon. The crew, including Flight Sergeant Jack Gadsby and Sergeant Eric Clarke, had been detailed to ferry Hampden P1826 back to Scampton, after it had been repaired. On the morning of the 17th, Pilot Officers Cooke and Manders had taken the Hampden up for a brief test flight alone, when the accident happened. News got back to Scampton that Gadsby and Clarke had also been killed, but this was incorrect.

Crashed Hampden, Pizze
P/O D COOKE: pilot   (killed)
P/O R MANDERS: pilot   (killed)

April 5th/6th, 1942: Bombing Cologne.

11 aircraft to bomb Cologne.

The attack on Cologne was scattered and stretched back across the city. Leaflets were also dropped within the target area. A night-fighter shot P/O Kay D.F.M. (AT156) and crew down over Philippeville, Belgium. The pilot and Sergeant Ainger were able to escape from the stricken aircraft to become POW, but Sergeants Bob Brown and Jim Waddell were sadly killed. They rest side by side in Charleroi Cemetery, Belgium.

FTR AT156
P/O KAY DFM:	pilot	(POW)
Sgt RWB BROWN:	air observer	(killed)
Sgt J WADDELL:	wireless operator & air gunner	(killed)
Sgt S AINGER:		(P.O.W)

April 6th/7th, 1942: Bombing Essen.

49 Squadron provided five aircraft for this raid. Three aircraft abandoned the raid due to icing, one reported bombing the primary target, but the fifth aircraft was reported missing. Flight Sergeant Leslie Davis (AT126) and crew are believed to have come down in the North Sea. The crew is remembered on the Runnymede Memorial. Four other aircraft were reported missing from the operation, one other Hampden, one Manchester, one Stirling and one Wellington.

FTR AT126
F/S L DAVIS:	pilot	(missing)
Sgt M GRIFFITHS:	wireless operator & air gunner	(missing)
Sgt C HARTLEY (RAAF):	as above	(missing)
Sgt D P WARMSLEY:	air observer	(missing)

Twentieth Operation: Bombing Essen, April 12th/13th 1942

HAMPDEN AD870
F/O ALCOCK: pilot
P/O WILLIAMS: navigator
SGT CLARK: wireless operator
SGT GAUNT: air gunner
Up 2135 hrs, down 0115 hrs (3 hrs 40 mins)

Details of Sortie: -
An unsuccessful sortie due to engine trouble. Bombs jettisoned in sea 10 miles west of Dunkirk in order to maintain height.

Summary of Events: -
Weather fine after early morning haze, wind light, southerly.

Shadows of the Past

12 aircraft detailed for operations, 11 bombing, one gardening.

11 aircraft took off for bombing and one took off 1 hour earlier for mining. Three aircraft attacked the alternative target, two attacked the primary and five had to abandon the operation due to engine trouble. One aircraft crashed on return at Fitling, Yorkshire, due to fuel shortage, three members of the crew killed. The pilot survived. All crews on bombing report, poor visibility with much haze, few results observed. Flares were observed in the target area. Of the aircraft which had to abandon the operation, one was attacked by an enemy fighter and sustained structural damage to the port main plane and port centre section.

Results: -
Disappointing series of raids on Essen.

Night April 12th/13th, 1942 – 251 aircraft in total, of which were 171 Wellingtons, 31 Hampdens, 27 Stirlings, 13 Halifaxes and nine Manchesters.

10 aircraft lost – 7 Wellingtons, two Hampdens, one Halifax.

173 aircraft claimed to have bombed Essen, but their bombing photographs showed many localities of the Ruhr. Essen's records show a slight improvement in the bombing, five high explosive and 200 incendiaries hit the Krupps factory and a large fire was started there, 28 private dwellings were destroyed and 50 seriously damaged, 27 people were killed, 36 injured and nine missing.

This raid concluded a disappointing series of raids on this target, which was judged to be the heart of the German armaments industry. There had been eight heavy raids since the first Gee raid on March 8th/9th– these were the conclusions: -

Aircraft dispatched 1555. Crews reported bombing Essen 1006. Aircraft lost 64. Aircraft bombing photographs showing ground detail 212. Aircraft bombing photographs within five miles radius of Essen 22.

Essen's records show that industrial damage was caused only on two occasions, a fire in the Krupps factory and a few bombs on some railway lines, that 63 civilians were killed and that a modest amount of residential property had been hit.

Other minor operations 58 sorties. Total effort for the night was 327 sorties, 10 aircraft lost (3.2%).

April 12th/13th, 1942: Bombing Essen.

After successfully bombing Essen, Sergeant Pilot James (AE196) and crew arrived back over England in the early hours of Monday, April 13th, desperately short of fuel, flying at 5,300 feet the engines suddenly cut out. The pilot gave the order to bale out before leaving the aircraft himself. Tragically, the remainder of the crew failed to get out in time and all three were killed in the crash. The Hampden dived to the ground at Chamberlain Charity Farm, Fitting, near Aldbrough in Yorkshire. The remainder of 49 Squadron returned safely to Scampton.

Crashed AT196
Sgt JAMES: pilot   (safe)
Sgt H TAYLOR: wireless operator & air gunner (killed)
Sgt J T SMITH: air gunner   (killed)
Sgt W J MARSHALL: air observer   (killed)

Unfortunately information about this was lost in Tubby's diary

April 14th/15th, 1942: Bombing Essen.

FTR AD931
P/O H G WILLIAMS: pilot   (P O W)
Sgt H S BROWN: wireless operator & air gunner (killed)
Sgt L W WEBBE: air observer   (killed)
Sgt W RALPH: air gunner   (P O W)

Twenty-first Operation: Bombing Dortmund, April 14th/15th, 1942

HAMPDEN AT191
Sgt FREEMAN: pilot
Sgt BUSH: navigator
Sgt GAUNT: wireless operator
Sgt AASH: air gunner
Up 2130 hrs, down 2301 hrs (2 hrs 1 min)

Tubby, end of first tour, April 1942.

Sgt Terry Freeman, end of tour, April 1942.

Details of Sortie: -
An unsuccessful sortie owing to engine trouble after reaching Honington.

Summary of Events: -
Weather fine, morning haze, wind S.E.

The squadron contributed seven aircraft to the main force attack on Dortmund, of these three returned early with engine failure. Three attacked alternative targets and one aircraft failed to return. The raid was very scattered, with bombs falling over a wide area of the Ruhr. Bomber command suffered the loss of five Wellingtons and four Hampdens.

Shadows of the Past

Pilot Officer Williams piloted the missing 49 Squadron Hampden. It is thought that he and his crew were caught by a night-fighter, which brought their aircraft down in Germany. The pilot and Sergeant Ralph, an air gunner, survived to become POWs. Sadly, Sergeants Horace Brown and Leslie Webbe were killed. They rest alongside each other in the *Reichwald* Forest cemetery at Kleve in Germany.

P/O H.G. WILLIAMS: pilot   (POW)
Sgt H.S. BROWN: wireless operator & air gunner   (killed)
Sgt L.W. WEBBE: air observer   (killed)
Sgt W. RALPH: air gunner   (POW)

Twenty-second Operation: Bombing Dortmund, 15th/16th April, 1942

HAMPDEN AT191
Sgt FREEMAN: pilot
Sgt BUSH: navigator
Sgt WELCH: navigator
Sgt GAUNT: air gunner
Up 2255 hr, down 0558 hrs (7 hrs 3 mins)

Details of Sortie: -
Last resort target attacked from 16,000 ft. at 0145 hrs. Aircraft iced up in target area and forced down, bombs believed to have fallen in vicinity of Bonn. Nickels released in area. Aircraft observed to be shot down in Ostend area at approx. 0033 hrs.

Summary of Events: -
Weather fine, wind light SE.
Six aircraft detailed for bombing operation and one for nickel operations. One aircraft took off for nickel operation, which was successfully carried out over the Lille area. Six aircraft took off for bombing operation at Dortmund. One successfully located the primary objective by concentration of Flak. No results observed. Nickels released in the area. Three aircraft located and attacked the alternative target. Bombs fell in built-up area. Flak and searchlights immediately engaging when bombs were released. Severe icing expcrienced near Bonn in thick cloud.

One aircraft unable to identify primary or alternative targets. Two captains observing aircraft shot down in vicinity of Ostend.

BCWD: -
152 aircraft despatched - 111 Wellingtons, 19 Hampdens, 15 Sterlings, seven Manchesters. Three Wellingtons and one Sterling lost.

Eight aircraft claimed to have bombed Dortmund, which reports that only the equivalent of eight bomb loads fell on Dortmund built up area.

Aircraft & Crew Losses

April 19th/20th, 1942: Minelaying.

On the evening Sunday, April 19th, 1942, the Squadron despatched three aircraft on a gardening operation to lay mines in the Terschelling area, all three Hampdens were airborne from Scampton by 2046 hrs heading for Ameland. Two aircraft carried out their sorties in very different conditions. Both crews were forced to carry out time and distance runs to plant their vegetables before returning to base.

The third aircraft was reported missing without trace. Sergeant Frank Slingo (AT217) and crew are believed to have come down in the North Sea of the Frisian Islands. On July 13th, the body of Flight Sergeant Ernie Jackson was washed ashore on the island of Rottumeroog and is buried in Sage War Cemetery near Oldenburg, Germany. The bodies of Sergeants Ian McLaren and Ray Webley were never found; they are remembered on the Runnymede Memorial.

They were the final Hampden crew to be lost by 49 Squadron during the Second World War.

FTR AT217
Sgt FW SLINGCO: pilot   (killed)
F/Sgt EW JACKSON: wireless operator & air gunner   (killed)
Sgt I McLAREN: air observer   (missing)
Sgt RJ WEBLEY: wireless operator & air gunner   (missing)

Shadows of the Past

Goodbye to the Hampdens.

The raid of April 23rd/24th, 1942, to Rostock was the last operation by 49 Squadron using Hampdens. Sergeant Hamer, Tubby's pilot on the Huls raid had the honour of being pilot in the last 49 Squadron Hampden crew to take off on an operational sortie. On Monday April 27th, all 49 Squadron Hampdens were transferred to 144 Squadron.

April finished on a sad note: no less than seven aircraft and all their gallant crews were lost. 49 Squadron were to carry out more Hampden sorties than any other squadron in 5 Group.

Hello to the Ambiguous Avro Manchester.

Late April 1942, 49 Squadron received a large influx of additional aircrew personnel, all trained on the Manchester, from 25 OTU, Finningley.

On Friday morning, May 1st, 1942, the posted strength of 49 Squadron stood at 29 officers and 655 airmen. Aircraft held on charge were 11 Avro Manchesters, which represented the operational equipment, with a further seven Manchesters awaited. The Squadron also held one Puss Moth and one Tiger Moth for training purposes. The next four months would see Tubby on conversion training, which started April 8th.

An example of a typical training Sortie, Skipper Wing Commander Stubbs: -
Hr   Aircraft   Pilot   Duty Self
1500   Manchester R772W/Com. Stubbs   Wireless Operator
The reputation of the Avro Manchester was appalling; it was everything the Hampden never was. The crews who flew this underpowered, troubled aircraft took an instant dislike to it. The mechanical problems were its hydraulic systems and generally the Rolls-Royce Vulture engines, which were just not man-enough for the job to be done. All too many sorties were being aborted. It was from this aircraft that the Lancaster was born, using four engines instead of two, the proven Merlin engines (as used on the Spitfire) powered this magnificent aircraft, which would take the brunt of Bomber Command's fight across to the mighty industrial cities of Germany.

Shadows of the Past 91

The Manchester was to be used for only about four months by 49 Squadron and the last operation that 49 Squadron Manchesters flew was the Bremen raid June 25th/26th, 1942. 960 aircraft assembled for this raid, losses were high - 52 aircraft lost, representing 5% of aircraft despatched. The heaviest losses were suffered by OTUs of 91 Group, which lost 23 aircraft from a total of 198 - 11.6%.

Tubby was to go through conversion on the Manchester, converting again onto the Lancaster, having not flown any operations on the Manchester. Conversion on the Manchester started April 8th, and finished on July 15th, 1942.

Conversion on the Lancaster started on August 4th, 1942, after just two days. With five hours and 25 minutes flying-time on Lancasters, Tubby was posted to 23 OTU Pershore, to train on Wellingtons as Staff W/Op; this posting was a stopgap. Tubby had applied to become a pilot, was accepted and spent six months at No 2 ITW, Cambridge. Before long, after a mid-air collision, he would be on a troopship taking him to South Africa to start his pilot's flying training.

May 19th, 1942
Conversion to the Avro Manchester
Mid-air Collision Over Grantham

Flying with Sergeant Freeman as wireless operator, Tubby and other crewmembers were settling in with the new aircraft when on the May 19th, 1942, during a night-time manoeuvre (dummy raid, searchlight co-operation) on London, their aircrft L7484 was in collision with a Lancaster of 83 Squadron, piloted by Squadron Leader Hinton The two aircraft, flying towards each other, touched wingtips. Damage to the Manchester was underside the starboard wing and the Lancaster lost its wingtip also starboard and outer engine stopped. Both aircraft landed safely at Scampton a few minutes later, to the relief of their respective crews.

Shadows of the Past 92

Tubby on a training sortie in Manchester L7398, June 1942.

Above left & below: snaps of the Isle of Sky, taken from the same Manchester and also on a training flight, April 1942.

S/L Peter de Mestre DSO DFC, 49 Sqn. One of Tubby's pilots, he was killed on June 7th, 1942, whilst converting from Hampdens to Manchesters.

HONOURS AND AWARDS

JANUARY 1942

P/O R J Robinson   DFC

FEBRUARY 1942

Sgt J C Price   DFM
Sgt J Mossop   DFM

MARCH 1942

F/O Walker   DFC
F/O Wood   DFC

(F/O Wood was killed at Finningley May 1942).

APRIL 1942

F/O R A P Allsbrook DFC
F/S T W Bell   DFM

MAY 1942

S/Ldr P M deMestre   DFC/DSO
S/Ldr P D S Bennett   DFC, Bar to DFC
F/Lt L P Massey   AFC/DFC
S/Ldr I O Hodges   DFC
F/Lt L F Ratcliff   DFC

More Pilot Training

With 5 hours 25 minutes flying time on Lancasters, Tubby was posted to 23 OTU Pershore as W/OP Staff Instructor. He would be there for one month from 8th August to 8th September 1942. He then moved to 14 OTU Cottesmore, again, as Staff Operator from 8th September to 19th October 1942. During this period of time Tubby had applied for pilot training. He was accepted and moved to No 2 ITW (Initial Training Wing) at Cambridge. His studies were carried out at (Maudling) University and practice flying at Marshals Airfield. On completion of

Shadows of the Past

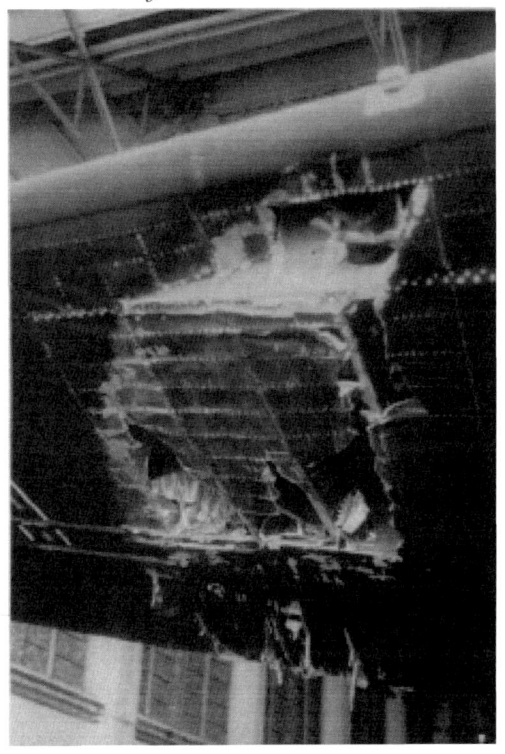

Damage to starboard wing of Manchester L7287, 'EA-G' (see page 91).

this training he was transferred to ACRC (Aircrew Reception Centre) Heaton Park, with draft 7713 South Africa. A troopship from Liverpool to Cape Town, South Africa, took from 17th June to 21st July 1943. From Cape Town, he moved to 2 PDC, 24 AS Witbank. Tubby was to train here for approximately 15 weeks, moving on to finish his pilot training at No 26 AS Petersburg, completing and gaining his wings and qualified to pilot twin engine medium bombers. This was to be the Wellington (X), the main medium bomber to be used in the Mediterranean theatre of war.

Tubby was the winner of the intake bombing trophy and can be seen proudly holding it in the photograph! He was immensely proud of his achievement and displayed the small replica cup on my mother's mantle shelf above the fireplace and it is still there today, 62 years later.

Stan Day Remembers

My pilot training was carried out in Rhodesia, our port of entry was Durban. The two troopships operating between Liverpool and Durban, South Africa were the Otranto and the Orontes. Each ship carried 5,000 personnel, Army, Navy, Air Force and nurses. These ships were of 25,000 Ton displacement. (Tubby's troopship was the liberty ship *George W Goethals* which sailed between Greenock and Cape Town.)

Shadows of the Past 95

No 2 ITW, main entrance to St John's New College, Cambridge, November 1942. Photo by Arthur Hornby, who appears on Tubby's right, 2nd left, front row.

Cape Town, from the Liberty Ship George W Goethals.

No 26 AS, St Petersburg, No 11 War Course, April 28th, 1944. End of training, Tubby front row with Intake Winner Trophy. Norman Moseley 4th left, top but one row standing, Howard Jones, 5th left, 2nd row. All three survived the war.

Shadows of the Past 96

Tubby receives his 'wings', April 28th, 1944.

Tubby receives 'Best of Intake' bombing trophy.

*Above: the trophy's inscription.
Right: a proud Tubby with trophy.*

'Wings Parade', April 28th, 1944.

When we sailed we had no idea where we were going, security prevented the troops from knowing the destination. Going out from England we sailed due west, we all thought we were going to America, then we turned south, to miss the Bay of Biscay round the U Boats. We lived 50 men to a mess deck, where we ate, slept and drank together. At night we would take out our hammocks and string them from hooks in the deck head and positioned our clews (piece of wood) at the head shoulder end, this kept the hammock open. During the day we packed all the hammocks away and sat around the mess tables. I personally spent most of my time on deck, singing, telling stories, playing cards, etc. We spent very little money, the only thing to buy were cigarettes. We did however play housy-housy (bingo) for 2p to 3p a game. The ablutions and showers were basic, showering with seawater is not recommended, as it felt sticky and it was difficult to lather the soap.

When our ship reached the Equator the ship's crew organised a huge crossing the line party. A small swimming pool was made from canvas and wood, one member of the crew in fancy dress acting as Neptune would dunk as many men as possible and present them with a certificate to prove their initiation and crossing.

Quastina Palestine, No 77 OTU

Leaving 26 AS South Africa, Tubby moved up through Africa, as a passenger in various aircraft, finally reaching Quastina on June 3rd. Here he met his crew and began training on the Wellington X. Maurice Sandell, Tubby's bomb aimer, remembers crewing up, as it was called, was carried out by bringing together an equal amount of aircrew in a room: 12 pilots, 12 rear gunners, 12 navigators, 12 bomb aimers, and 12 wireless operators (the front gunner would be a spare 'bod' to complement the six man crew). The crewing up party was simple: a pilot met a navigator, who knew a bomb aimer, and just chatted together. It was not long, may be half an hour, and all the crews were self selected and started the rapport that would, with training, make them a happy crew and effective fighting unit. Ten weeks of training at the OTU gave the new crew a thorough insight into the Wellington X, and on September 10th, the crew flew into Foggia and joined 37 Squadron.

New pilots arrive at No 77 OTU, Tubby centre, top row, Howard Jones 2nd right, front row.
Photo: Howard Jones.

Chapter Five

Foggia (Tortorella)
37 Squadron, 'B' Flight, CMF, No 205 Group

It was October 17th, when Tubby and his crew arrived at Tortorella. The conditions in which they would be both living and operating were totally different from those at Scampton, where there were cosy billets with central heating radiating warmth around the beds, drying and airing clothes and smalls - what a cosy life!

The city of Foggia is situated on the east side of Italy, 50 miles north of Bari and 15 miles inland of Manfredonia on the Adriatic coast. The large flat areas around Foggia were perfect for the quick building of airfields for the Allied air forces. No 205 Group was based on the Foggia plain.

No 231 Wing with 37 and 70 Squadrons was based at Tortorella, which was known as 'Foggia 2'.

No 236 Wing with 40 and 104 Squadrons was based at 'Foggia Main'. This was actually the Group's only permanent airfield throughout the war.

No 330 Wing with 142 and 150 Squadrons was based at Cerignola and Torretta (known as 'Cerignola No 3'), then Amendola, later moving to Regina, near San Severo in July 1944.

No 240 Wing was at Celone. No 614 Squadron was at Stornara and later moved to Amendola on July 15th, coming under the command of No 240 Wing.

Tents were the only shelter for most of the air and ground crews; the odd farm house gave shelter to the more senior ranks (37 Squadron camped in an olive grove and most of 70 Squadron were in a wheat field). Conditions were generally not good.

Shadows of the Past 100

Above: Frank 'Geordie' Hazelden, Tubby's rear gunner, 3rd from left in front of an Avro Lincoln, Scampton, 1952.

Top left: Dave 'Jock' Scanlon, Tubby's navigator.

Top right: Maurice 'Scats' Scandell, Tubby's bomb aimer.

Left: Geordie Hazelden today, Golden Beach, Australia.

Pilot Officer Bill Hunt
Foggia Main 1944/45: A Navigator Recalls

'I don't know whether the winter was colder and wetter than usual for that part of Italy, but there was certainly a lot of bad weather, with the Squadron being stood down for days at a time on account of low cloud, driving rain and poor visibility, not only in the Foggia Plain but over most of Italy, the Balkans and Austria. The wind howled through the Manfredonia Gap and drove rain like a shower of needles horizontally across the land. The officers' and sergeants' messes were established in farm buildings and were comfortable in a spartan sort of way. The CO had his caravan which also served as an office, the flight commanders and one or two other officers, such as the squadron medical officer, had rooms in the farmhouse. The tents the rest of us had to sleep in were rather old and decrepit, which I suspect had seen service in the North African desert and getting decidedly worse for wear.

'To make things more comfortable many people made improvements to their tents, digging out a little and making wooden sides with timber scrounged from the Americans who shared the airfields and who had vast quantities of packing cases in which their spares for aircraft and road transport came. Many air and ground crews heated their tents by means of home-made stoves. These were usually referred to as 'drip feeds', because of the principle of operation. The basic requirements were a metal pan, fairly shallow, a container of some sort to act as a reservoir for the diesel line fuel, some metal tube and a tap or stopcock. Then a similar provision was required to introduce water to the pan. Sand was put in the pan, fuel added, and with luck this could be induced to burn after lighting. I don't pretend to understand the physics of the contraption, but adding water made it burn all the more fiercely and I suppose at a higher temperature. The aircraftsmen that had skill in metalwork and access to materials and tools had vastly superior installations, some of which had to be seen to be believed. You may think that they were highly dangerous devices, and so they were. Every few weeks there would be a tent fire during the night. I don't think anyone was badly hurt, but there was a court of enquiry into the incident. No one, so far as I know, ever got into serious trouble over these fires.

Shadows of the Past

Bill Hunt visited the Foggia airfields in 1992, finding a section of PSP (Pierced Steel Planking), which made possible the building of improvised runways.

*Wellington on a training flight from Quastina.
Photo: Ron Cooper.*

'The cold was usually a raw, damp cold. There was little frost.

'We did have some snow one day when I was still on 34 SAAF Squadron, very early January. Some of the South Africans had never seen snow and while the RAF chaps were huddled around the fire in the mess complaining, the SAAF (South African Air Force) boys were outside, some stripped to the waist, enjoying a colossal snowball fight. There were the odd mornings too, when I recall having to break the ice which had formed in the jerry can in which we kept water so that we could shave, but this was unusual.

'The worst thing created by the elements was mud. In summer, the Foggia plain had been baked hard as iron, and every wind blew fine dust everywhere. By the time I arrived in the area, middle October 1944, the autumn rains had set in, the dust was laid and mud was king. Our usual transport was three-ton trucks, and these slithered about the makeshift roadways in an alarming manner. The mud in places was over the wheel hubs. Walking anywhere was a matter of difficulty and the aircraft inside were covered with mud when crews embarked. We had been issued with Wellington boots, but seldom wore them because they were so cold to the feet. Instead we wore our suede flying boots and inside of these a pair of seaboot stockings. The boots were very loose fitting around the leg and diabolically awkward to walk in, but at least we could keep our feet warm. How the erks fared I really can't say, it was a great advantage having flying kit.

'Most of the crews wore our quilted inner flying suits under battle dress the whole time, we even slept in them. The bathing arrangements were primitive, once a week a truck took us to Foggia, to the bombed out swimming baths, where a sort of shower facility had been rigged up. There was a long metal pipe with holes in it at intervals, somewhere there was a boiler, which fed scalding hot water into the pipe, one stood beneath one of the holes and while trying to avoid the water falling directly on to the skin, caught a few drops on a flannel and soaped oneself. Removing the soap was an even trickier business, one crouched down as near the floor as possible to maximise the cooling effect on the water of its descent through the air.

Shadows of the Past 104

At Foggia Main, 1944/45, mud was king, conditions appalling. All photos this page, & top two facing page, by John King.

Shadows of the Past

Bomb damage: Foggia, 1944.
Photo: Matt Muir.

'Shower day was also laundry day; one called first at a farmhouse, whose ladies took in our washing, to collect clean shirts, socks and underwear, then to the showers for the uncomfortable ablutions and returned to the farmhouse with the dirty linen. During the winter, underwear was seldom removed at all between showers. One week a number of crews were on daylight operations on shower afternoon and that time, I have to confess, I went a whole fortnight without taking off my clothes.

'Food was fairly indifferent, but in the officer's mess, certainly the rations were made more appetising from the American Sergeants' mess. It appears that hard liquor was not permitted for the American forces enlisted men and for a half a case of scotch from the mess ration, the Yanks would fill a fifteen hundredweight truck with all sorts of good things, from Spam to ring doughnuts (Tubby had his eye on an American aircrew flying jacket, that cost him 1 bottle of scotch and very little negotiating). The American food contribution made a most welcome change from bully beef and fritters and a vile concoction called M&V. This stood for meat and veg; it came in tins and had a hauntingly horrible flavour caused, it was said, by the inclusion of potatoes in the mixture. Whether the Sergeants' messes had similar arrangements with their opposite numbers in the American camps I cannot say, but I would be surprised if it were not so.

'In the messes there was not much of an Englishmen's usual tipple to be had: a very small ration of bottled Canadian beer; perhaps two bottles a month each in the officer's mess. My "skip" and I used to save ours up and share a bottle now and then after getting back from an operation.

'The rest of the time we drank a frightful rotgut Italian wine, known officially as Lacrima Cristi and irreverently by the RAF as 'Jesus Wept'. Sometimes we drank gin, whisky was rather scarce, most of it having been traded with the Yanks, and there was a sort of tacit understanding that one left it for some of the older men - the CO and so forth. Not that I drank whisky in those days, so it seemed no hardship. We would have given a great deal for a pint of good English bitter now and then though.

*Excellent end of tour photo beside Wellington 'Flak Harry':
Doug Skinner's crew, 104 Sqn, Foggia Main, 1945. From
left: Wilf Eardley (nav), Charlie Williams (A/G), Jack Grey
(W/Op), Doug Skinner (pilot), Jim Sterret (bomb aimer).
Photo: the late Doug Skinner.*

*Sgts Sexton, Harry Richmond, Charlie Louch, Ringstell & ground staff
with Wellington X 'Scourge of the Balkans', which completed 35
bombing sorties, one mining and five supply drops, Foggia, 1944.*

Shadows of the Past
Bill Hunt Remembers
the Wellington Bomber

'The Wellington was affectionately known as the 'Wimpey' by the crews who flew this workhorse of a bomber. The immense strength of the fuselage was due to its geodetic structure. The outer skin was doped fabric for lightness. Most crews loved and had a deep affection for the Wellington. It was a tremendously reliable aircraft and it was a rare thing that problems caused an early return from operations. The final Mark X Wellington would cruise at 150 mph with a full load and return at 170 mph empty. It was capable of flying at 255 mph. The heating system was primitive, it was almost impossible to maintain any suitable temperature for all the crew. The engines were two Bristol Hercules each delivering 1650 hp, each with two speed superchargers, giving maximum power at 7,000 feet and 14,000 feet. The power enabled the aircraft to take off and climb very well. The maximum all up weight (AUW) was approaching 3,6000 lb. With main tanks full, the Wellington carried 4,500 lb of bombs beside guns and ammunition. Operations close to base enabled the bomb load to reach 6,500 lb, with reduced fuel in the tanks.Targets a greater distance away could be reached using over load tanks, but a smaller bomb load was carried.

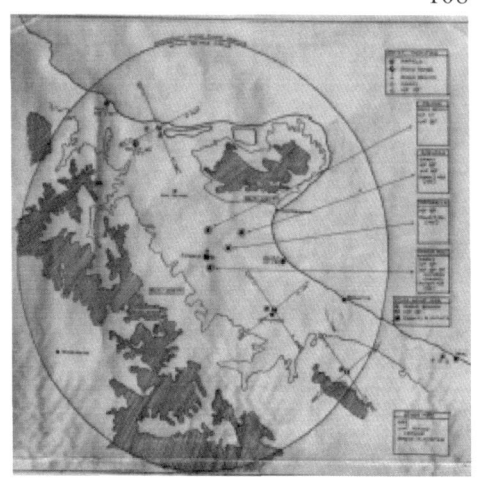

Chart showing airfields on the Foggia Plain, & various radio beacon 'Darky' facilities & other navigational aids.

'The Wellington was armed with six .303 Browning machine-guns and had a general range (carrying 4,500 lb of bombs) of 1,325 miles.

'The aircraft unfortunately was rather prone to ignition; aircraft crash-landing nearly always burst into flames and were completely destroyed. Tubby's aircraft, when it crash landed in the Yugoslav mountains, did

Shadows of the Past 109

not burn after the crash landing, probably because it broke almost in two and scraped up a belly-full of snow, which covered the entire crash site some two – three feet deep.

What was it like going on ops?

'How did we, as crew members, feel before going on operations? This is perhaps the most difficult question of all. In those war days the culture of the stiff upper lip prevailed, it is to me and perhaps to many of my generation, quite incomprehensible that media persons, with apparent

Sgt Norman Moseley & crew, 37 Sqn, Tortorella (Foggia). From left: Peter Boulton (nav), Bill Ward (W/Op), Moseley (pilot), John Bell (bomb aimer), John Flockhart (rear gunner). Photo: Norman Moseley.

Shadows of the Past

insensitivity, microphone in hand, demand of the recently bereaved, "But how did you feel, Mrs. Robinson, when they told you your husband and two children had been killed by a drunken driver?".

'We had our feelings, of course, but we suppressed them. This was necessary in the interest of morale. The thing was neatly summed up by a colleague after the war who referred to the days when, "Death was something you didn't talk about, that happened to other people". This suppression of emotions was, I think, a factor in making recall, especially at this distance of time, difficult. I dare say that some people would still feel that to ask the question is to attempt to enter forbidden territory. However, I have no inhibitions about that, but no very clear recollections either. We went to 'flights' each morning, segregated by our functions, not as crews. That is, navigators went to the navigation section brief, wireless operators to their hut, and so on. After a time, a list would appear with crews for the night's ops, or sometimes afternoon's operation. Or, of course, there would be news of a stand down, usually because of extremely bad weather. If ones crew were on the 'battle order', I seem to recall a slight feeling which might be best described as a mixture of excitement and anxiety; but it was not a very strong emotion. One affected to take things in one's stride and as a navigator one had at once to address one's-self to the practical aspects of the matter. There was a laid down route to be flown, and a flight plan to be drafted out.

'A time for the operation briefing would be announced, after which there was not much time to worry about the probability of things.

'Before briefing, one put one's flying kit on, plenty of warm clothing under battledress, flying boots, an Irvine jacket if one had been lucky enough to get one (there never seemed enough to go round in Italy). Then when briefing was complete, out to the three-ton truck which would take several crews out to their respective aircraft dispersals.

'At some stage, one put on the Mae West life jacket and parachute harness. Parachutes were drawn from the stores for each flight and returned afterwards. Rear gunners usually wore their side flying suits on top of everything else except the Mae West and harness; rear turrets were very icy and draughty. They also wore silk gloves inside the leather gauntlets, which were part of the standard issue of flying kit. I could not work in gloves, but found that woollen mittens, knitted by some kind lady in England, kept the hands warm while leaving the fingers free. In Liberator bombers, which the squadron went on to in February 1945, there were facilities for plugging electrically heated suit and some air gunners were issued with these.

'Once in the aircraft, one put on the flying helmet, from which dangled the oxygen mask fitted with a microphone. The headphones were in the helmet and one plugged in an intercom lead to check the equipment.

'However, before boarding the aircraft, there were usually a few minutes to spare and if there was still some daylight, we would walk about, joking about something or other, perhaps indulging in a little mutual chaff or mild horseplay and stopping alongside the forward landing wheels for a final 'nervous pee' before boarding - I do not think we ever speculated about the operation that lay ahead. Everyone had some sort of pre-flight check to carry out and this helped to suppress any nervousness one might feel. Once the engines were started, there was plenty to occupy the attention and this was focused on the immediate moment, not on what might lie ahead. We had, it must be remembered, very little flying experience and the very fact of flying was still in itself something of an adventure.

'Even approaching the target, while one might have a momentary feeling of butterflies in the stomach, there was too much to concentrate on to allow time for worrying about the possibility of disaster. It may have been different for those who had had bad previous experiences, but I was lucky and although not cast in a very heroic mould, had the necessary confidence that the worst simply wasn't going to happen to me. As it turned out, I was right, of course.

'This frame of mind, though totally unfounded in reason, was almost a necessary condition of operational flying. What things must have been like in Bomber command in the early days of the war, or even 205 group during the summer of 1944, I cannot imagine. True, we continued to have losses from time to time, but not to the extent that we ever questioned our probability of survival.

Shadows of the Past

'While on this subject, it may be apposite to touch on the question of superstition. I suspect that some men had private and secret superstitions that others never heard of - never flying without taking some item a girlfriend had given them, for instance. I am not personally superstitious to any great extent and if I sometimes say 'touch wood' when something is in the balance, I like to think this is more a verbal habit than a serious attempt to influence the outcome of some matter in my favour. Even so, what has been called 'the long arm of coincidence' was sometimes apparent in operational matters.

'While I was on 70 Squadron at Tortorella, we had, I think, twenty aircraft. The usual thing was to give each aircraft on a squadron an identifying letter and for 'A' flight to have the first half of the alphabet, while 'B' flight's aircraft started from N. Now it happened before my time on 70 Squadron, that six aircraft had been lost over a short period of time. Three were lettered G-George and three T-Tommy. At this point, someone made the decision not to use these letters on the next replacement aircraft to arrive and the letters K and X were used instead. I imagine that crew members had commented on the coincidence and because of the possibility that this might be a 'worrying factor' which could, albeit unconsciously, predispose to disaster, the powers that be, perhaps the squadron CO, decided to play safe.

'Another odd thing I noticed about this affair is that G and T were each the seventh aircraft in their respective flights. Bill asks was Tubby's aircraft that crashed in Yugoslavia numbered likewise.

Coincidentally, yes, G for George LP614! Some time after the war, Bill was talking to a fellow navigator, who said that on his station they had a WAAF whom none of the aircrew would date. Apparently several had done so and in each case had been killed on operations shortly after. The unfortunate girl was referred to not, I hope, to her face - as a chop-WAAF. If you dated her you were lined up for the chop.

The trouble with superstition is that while no one can prove that there is any substance in it, no one can prove that there is not.

Tubby's wife, Florence, knitted an air force blue scarf that was a suitable size. Tubby wore it throughout the war during operations, except one particular day, January 8th 1944. Again, was this purely coincidence?

Bill concludes: -

'One matter with regard to our feelings I can be sure about; we were perhaps without exception, very homesick. One chore, which developed upon officers, was censoring the other rank's mail for forbidden references to places, units and operations. On the back of envelopes there sometimes appeared cryptic words like SWALK (sealed with a loving kiss), but far more often there were simply the letters ROTB - roll on the boat, the troopship, that is to say that takes me home. We, of course, had no WAAFs to date and that was no doubt part of the trouble. The longing for the homeward-bound boat even appeared in the words of an RAF song'.

Chapter Six

Flight Sergeant Bob Foster
Rear Gunner
(Who Flew With Tubby Once)

As war broke out, Bob was attending Riverdale Collegiate in Toronto. In 1942 he left school; all he wanted to do was to emulate his father, who was a First World War pilot. He was disappointed when he applied at the recruiting office: he was rejected and offered air gunnery. Bob was not a happy man and objected, but was subsequently told he would have a ground trade if he did not accept gunnery. Reluctantly Bob accepted, and was soon at MontJoli - home of No 9 Bombing and Gunnery School. He arrived in the autumn of 1943, the school being the largest of 10 B&G schools, having 1,000 staff and 600 students. Nearly all had turrets for air-to-air firing (the targets were drogues towed by other Battles and Nomads).

The course was only six weeks ground school and six weeks of air firing. Bob had a close friend who was tragically killed in a mid-air collision on the last morning of his air schooling.

Bob went on to finish first in his class (winning the Skeet shooting trophy). He received his air gunner's beret on November 11th 1943; they were presented to him by his father, Lieutenant Harry J Foster.

Foster was soon on his way to England and to No 26 OTU at Winey, Buckinghamshire. He did a few operations dropping Nickels and during one trip to Paris was astounded when his Wimpey was pummeled by flak; he never thought anyone would actually shoot at him! After a short period in India, Foster was posted to 142 Squadron at Cerignola for a few days, only to be posted to 37 Squadron, where he met Tubby. Soon on operations, Foster would sometimes be spare bod (front or rear gunner) mainly to build up his experience and confidence – when a spare bod was required by a crew, it was totally on a volunteer basis.

Shadows of the Past

Sgt Bob Foster (left) with his father, Canada, 1943, who was the Station Commander & presented Bob with his A/G brevet.

Bob Foster (2nd left, top) with Sgt Duncan & other aircrew in London, 1944.

Bob Foster & an u/k aircrew, Tortorella olive grove, 1944.

The grave of Sgt Duncan, Bob's pilot, Bari, Italy, November 15th, 1945.

The now late Bob Foster (2nd right) with his fellow barber shop singers, 1996.

On November 25th, a couple of weeks after flying as a rear gunner for Tubby, Foster was flying with his regular crew on a raid with two other Wimpeys. Coming home he realised the pilot was having difficulty controlling the aircraft. A Mosquito came up from behind and signaled that he wanted to 'play a bit'. Foster signaled negative, they were in trouble. The Mosquito escorted them back to Tortorella, where on landing the Wimpey pitched up, crashed and exploded. Foster was still alive and tried to escape through the fuselage, but the heat and flames beat him back. Closing his hatch he started to drift into euphoria, flames all around he screamed for help. Outside the whole area was an inferno, the aircraft had blown up in the dispersal area, other aircraft were burning and explosions were numerous. Two ground crew who had fled to the trenches heard Foster and ran across to drag him through a small panel in the turret. Although badly burned and with a damaged leg, Foster would be healed within a few months. His four crewmen were all killed in the crash and are buried in the commonwealth war graves at Bari, Southern Italy.

Shadows of the Past

Foster later met his rescuers, who joked that it was because they were tired of his screams that they pulled him free. The two airmen were:
>14433911 CPL Smith ARMR 37 SQDN
>1417240 LAC Williams FMA 37 SQDN

Both the ground crew involved were commended for their action.

Footnote: -
I had the pleasure of meeting the sadly now late Bob Foster in October 1992, in Toronto, where he ran a very successful automobile dealership with his son. His location in Scarborough, Toronto, is famed for the large RCAF ensign, which flies over the building.

Bob was, like me, pleased that we had met and on my return to England he presented me with the book, The Royal Canadian Air Force at War 1939-45. He said that he wanted to write something in remembrance of my late father, "he thought something flowery, no", Tubby was not a flowery person, so he wrote, "In remembrance of a true gentleman of the air force, a professional and a friend, Philip Henry Tubby Gaunt. Bob Foster ex-Air Gunner 37 Sqn 2.10.92".

Tubby Gaunt & Crew
by
Dave Scanlan, Sergeant Navigator

Quastina, No 77 OTU, Palestine.
I have not many memories of training at Quastina; we were a very efficient crew and a happy crew at that. I made many friendships among other navigators. We were very much Tubby Gaunt's crew and we went about together. One weekend, with a two-day pass, we went to Tel Aviv for a couple of days enjoyment.

At Quastina, our crew stayed in the same hut and if we had no money, we would pass the time playing cards and cribbage, no bets though. I usually partnered your father (Tubby).

Shadows of the Past

'Geordie' (Sergeant Hazeldin)

He was an ex-army truck driver in North Africa and came over to the RAF as an air gunner, taking a six-week course as rear gunner. Geordie was a salt-of-the-earth rough diamond; he helped to keep the crew alive and would scrounge food from 'who knows where' on a continual basis (we didn't ask where).

Dave, Scats, and Mac were 21 years old: Tubby was much older, in actual fact he was 27 in 1944. Geordie was 23. Dave actually thought Tubby was about 30ish. Tubby never said a harsh word about anyone and to my mind was a very agreeable person.

Foggia

When we arrived at Foggia, we had two kit bags, one held flying kit helmet and mask and the other our Khaki wet weather uniform, shorts, shirts, etc.

Arriving at Foggia 17-10-44, Tortorella, food was awful. An NCO met us at Tortorella; he gave us two scratchy, itchy blankets and a palliasse, this being a material type mattress that had to be filled with straw. He took us to the barn and told us what to do. We were then told to go and find a tent and that one person went in one, and two in another, this was the first time our crew was split up.

After searching for some time, looking in tent after tent and being told to 'sod off', I eventually walked into one that had a vacancy and announced that my name was Jock and proceeded to settle in, whether they liked it or not. I was very despondent and conditions were just 'awful'.

On May 7th 1943, my brother died in a flying accident near Birmingham. I was very upset and despondent and was concerned about my performance as a navigator. I was not a gung ho type and the conditions were rotten, but accepted the situation.

Tubby made friends with the Americans on the other side of the airfield. The runway was pierced steel planking which interlocked together, the mud just oozed through and when we got a lift, the truck frequently got stuck and we had to push it out, 16 of us at a time.

At meal times, we had two rounds of bread; the other food was just terrible. The Sgts. Mess had so much scotch whisky and this was traded to the Americans for two trays of doughnuts per day, we were allowed two or three doughnuts each per day, also once a day we were allowed a slice of what one can only described as cake. Quite a different consistency, like a solid ginger cake; this, the doughnuts and tea kept us alive. One lunchtime I met a young pilot on his way to lunch. He asked me what we were having to eat. Potatoes I said, usual mush - this turned him off and he turned and walked back to his tent. It bothered me the way this state of affairs was allowed to persist, that this pilot and probably most pilots would be on operations that evening and would not have a proper meal inside them. The Americans across the airfield ate the most delightful meals, three times a day, every day, perhaps Tubby's fraternising with them had another reason. When we were invited to the P.X. American NAAFI, we filled our stomachs with as much food as was possible and took back all we could reasonably carry.

Tubby one day was given a jeep to take us back to our tents, this we kept for some time. Tubby was quite a driver. We skidded the jeep so accurately within 3 inches of our tent. We went over to the PX three times a week. Tubby fell in with the American Ground Crew. Their tent was dug in the ground, with proper bunks, switch lights, and radios. The British Commonwealth Air Crew thought the Americans were spoilt, but I blamed the British Government for our very poor food and living conditions; how we operated so professionally with our poor back up at base amazes me.

'Tubby'
Asking Dave for his reactions to my father as a leader (skipper), his reply was, 'Just a super guy; put a white beard and a red suit on him and he would be just perfect as Santa Clause". 9½ hours at Grading School told me I would not be a good pilot as I had a nervous disposition. Tubby was just coolness personified - today's American 'Mr Cool'.

Crash-landing
13,000 feet, stalled, pulled out at 8000 feet. Keep stalling speed by keeping nose up slightly. This lasted for 10-15 minutes, safety height 10,000 feet, loosing height all the time. In cloud - mountains, 6,000

Shadows of the Past

feet, should bail out. I suggested this; Tubby said we would stick together, as it was, this turned out for the best. We continued to fall due to the ice - 7,500 feet - 7,000 feet - 6,500 feet - 6,000 feet - 5,000 feet - 4,500 feet - 3,800 feet - altimeter last reading. Someone up front called out "ground below", almost instantly Tubby put the nose down. Frank, the rear gunner, said land on both sides, we were flying down a valley - broke clear of cloud, south, south east, the mountains were 5,500 feet. Pilots were supposed to be strapped into their seats, unfortunately Tubby was not. After we stalled and pulled out, he dare not let go of the controls to buckle up, so he had to do without his safety belt. Despite a perfect wheels up belly landing, Tubby was thrown forward into the windshield and badly bruised and cut his forehead.

The next day, I went back to the stricken aircraft and sure enough, a panel in the screen was broken and pushed out. I put my hand through the hole where Tubby's forehead had hit it; fortunately he had no serious injury. I smashed the Gee box green radar tube as much as possible, although I thought the Germans by now would be well acquainted with this piece of equipment.

We spent a couple of days in Gerovo before moving off in a south easterly direction. I remember the partisans being dressed in British battledress and greatcoats with their green forage caps and red star. No doubt the uniforms were taken from the stricken Wellington's containers.

<u>Bombing Runs</u>
Scats had said that Tubby did not like going over the target a second time, although on more than three or four low level operations we had to go round three or four times dropping two or three bombs at a time on various targets on the mountain roads. On one operation, with Flight Lieutenant Cooke present in the aircraft, he asked that each time we went round on a bombing run to go lower and lower, to obtain more accurate results and bring the front and rear guns to accurate fire against the retreating Germans. The low level bombing raids were against motor transport and troop concentrations on the mountain, in target areas such as Stenica Priboj — Visegrad Prijipoli - Bugojno and Uzice town. Sometimes three squadrons would be on such operations; the overall effect was devastating, causing immense damage to motor transport and

death and injury to German infantry. These raids were organised with the help of the Partisans on the ground. Nickels were dropped during each of these raids.

Nickels - Leaflets
These were full of information for the civilians, not to join or help the Germans. Dave went on to say that the Tito Partisans were told that all the supply and bombing raids were being carried out by Russian aircraft and such was the level of education (could not read), they firmly believed this, the majority of supplies were dropped by the British, using Halifax and Wellington aircraft. They would not know a British aircraft from a Russian one. This was possibly some of the first communist propaganda.

Gerovo
Soon after we crash landed, we were met by the locals and partisans in uniform, who treated us very well, sharing with us both warmth and shelter and what food they could. At one of our brief two - three day stops, we met a British officer in charge of the local mission, Captain Harrison, whom we visited each day for information and some supplies. Food was scarce, cigarettes were more abundant and although we did not all smoke, we said we did and would obtain cigarettes for bartering purposes, to obtain food, if any, from the locals. The purpose of these missions was to work with the partisans, obtaining information on the organisation and coordination for supply drops and best military targets, such as the low level bombing and strafing operations against the retreating Germans.

Slunj – Zadar
The mission at Slunj - the officer offered us money for anything personal or not, that we had lost, sold or bartered during and after the crash for food. Tubby was the only one to obtain payment for his silver cigarette case he had exchanged for food, a payment of £10 - we let him off lightly. The last three nights were spent at a house, which was occupied by a grandmother, daughter and almond faced children - boy of 12, girl of 11 and a baby. Coarse grain maize corn was ground and made into porridge (polenta) or finely ground for bread making. An unpleasant memory was the bad habit everyone had of spitting. They all spat, mother, daughter, even the baby spat on his mattress on the floor. I used that as

Shadows of the Past

an educational purpose how human nature habits can be passed on (after the war Dave became a teacher in Canada).

The Partisan with us at the time had been shot in the ankle and although he was in pain, he never complained. I enjoyed borrowing their skis and made one or two runs down the hills. The timber they cut was very neatly stacked and in varying sections, to dry and use in the stoves.

Slunj
No British mission, no cigarettes, but there were sticks of tobacco that were sliced off with a razor - rolled in newspaper/magazine paper.

DRAVO - Good day, Good morning, Good evening.

PADOBRAN was the Croatian name for parachute.

The crew took their parachutes with them, as they were much sort after. A segment of parachute could be exchanged for almost anything and as food was the priority, most, if not all, the chutes were exchanged and some for cigarettes, or for a night's rest – these good people would have been shot had the Germans found out.

The villages and towns we went through would have plenty of apples or nuts, but not both. Some villages, although less than 7 miles apart, would only have what they grew. Transport between them was none existent, food did not move about. The locals would live almost only on one or the other, they either grew it, had it, or nothing at all. While at Slunj, we managed to buy a chicken, which was wonderful, and we made sure some was left for a second day. Upon going to prepare what was left, we found just a carcass, someone, we think the cook, had enjoyed some pickings.

Whilst at Slunj we were joined by an American liberator crew who had force-landed due to fuel shortage and they were to be taken with us on to Koronica, where lorries would take us down to Zada.

February 9th recalled getting back to Foggia.

Shadows of the Past

Foggia Tortorello
Our washing would be done by locals for five cigarettes a week.

We were a happy lot - in the Sergeants' Mess we would drink the local wine and listen to Foggia radio. We made our own radios by using razorblades and use our own flying helmet headsets.

We played soccer and the Squadron's CO, Wing Commander Langham, was a pleasant boss - he even let me borrow his football boots on one occasion!

Operations
On the low level attacks on the German infantry, Flight Lieutenant Cooke had us attacking from about 500 - 600 feet, with both front and rear gunners belting away at the troop concentrations on the roads below, causing catastrophic damage and death.

Tubby and Cooke were so calm and matter-of-fact. The danger situation just did not become a factor in the very professional way in which attack after attack was carried out. Compared with a tour over Germany, with heavy anti-aircraft fire and fighters attacking, to Tubby and Cooke, this was a piece of cake/stroll in the park.

Korenica – Captain Harrison
Miro injured foot (shot).
The two young Dutch lads (press-ganged into German navy).
Tubby led by appearing not to lead. If there was a problem he would suggest ways of overcoming the difficulty.
Tubby was like a captain and centre-half of a football team.
Tubby was well above average, he led by suggesting ways of overcoming a problem, he was not a bossy person and he was able to overcome problems before they happened.

Naples – Potechi
Transportation of goods/food was rare during wartime and between small villages, was non-existent.
Foggia - Cigarettes 50 free, others were duty free.

Shadows of the Past
Dave Scanlan Remembers

How did you feel when you were looking back? Well; I felt generally fine, I enjoyed it, I think. I am no storybook hero. I must admit, I didn't like the low level troop attacks, I just hated them. ACK, ACK was very frightening. Some said ACK ACK was more frightening at night rather than day, but I thought otherwise. At night, tiny fireworks flaring up and disappearing during the day, ACK ACK would explode and leave patches of smoke and to fly through these recently exploded shells was very (intimidating) frightening. On the ground in Jugoslavia I felt fine, in the air I was not as comfortable. I took my boots off in the tent and not entirely in jest; I said these used to be my flying boots!

When we walked through the enemy lines, I thought, would the Germans attack us if we were discovered, or would they be content to keep their heads down, not wanting to attack an unknown number of armed partisans, remembering that they were the retreating, beaten army. Just hoping to get through Jugoslavia and nearer to home, as safely as possible, capture meant certain death unless you were a fairly high-ranking officer who could be exchanged for partisan prisoners. I was not particularly afraid while passing through the German lines, but was relieved when our courier said we could walk slower and relax a little, as the main danger was passed.

I was an amateur footballer before the war in civvy street and would sometimes play the game all day and back at the Squadron I played when I could, so physically I was very fit and able to withstand the arduous trek back to safety, but ever since this experience, I do not like the cold, although it didn't seem to bother me at the time.

Looking back, I quite enjoyed escaping - it was an adventure I will always remember. I was not at all at my wits end and cannot ever remember saying to myself, this is awful, I can't stand it any more, so I was fairly comfortable, certainly happier on the ground than dodging the flack and bullets in the air.

Shadows of the Past

Just before leaving Foggia for home, the Italian lira was devalued by 100%, so doubling our exchange money from 400 lira to 800 lira to the English pound, unfortunately we were only there a further two weeks and so we could not make use of it like our fellow crews. We were to be sent home on survival leave and as such, were looking forward to seeing our families - Tubby had been away for nearly two years.

The troopship took about 10 days from Naples to Liverpool, all the troops on reaching Liverpool were jubilant and disembarked. We were repatriated prisoners and so had to stay on board a further night to our disappointment.

Last night on the troopship
We played cards and drank a bottle of plonk which we purchased in Naples.

Back home in Glasgow, I was given a desk job, just ten minutes from where I lived and later went back to Quastina until the end of the war.

Tent at Foggia
In the tent at Foggia, we had a drip feed fire that kept us warm.

Geordie
Stole bread, we toasted on stove.

Many tents went up in flames, the drip feed fires were dangerous - I never heard of anyone being disciplined. Bedding and equipment were lost in these fires.

A group of Australians around the base scrounged a jeep to carry materials and built themselves a cabin out of materials from here and there. Their beds were made of intertwined cable; this made a far better bed than the standard pallyass. We were invited to the Australian cabin for a little party at Christmas, they had cakes sent from Australia and 100% proof spirit that came in Aspirin bottles, Tubby got on with everyone and we were fortunate to be two of very few who had been invited to the party, this was entirely due to Tubby's way of getting on with every nationality.

Shadows of the Past

What a lovely party we had. We also acquired some Italian whisky - it was not drinkable.

We poured this whisky down the mouse holes and put a match to it. These mice soon ate our short supplies of bread, sometimes we would watch two or three of them, mesmerised for two or three minutes at a time.
It was at that time whilst shaving outside the tent, using our metal mirrors, we saw Bob Foster's plane go and blow up in the dispersal area.

The local Italian barber would cut our hair, it took about 30 minutes each and if there was half a dozen of us waiting, it still took him 30 minutes for each person, so sometimes we could wait two or three hours for our turn. He charged 10 or 20 lira.

Dave
My daughter asked me how long we had known each other – not quite 9 months, not long but so much happened to us.

Bill Hunt Recalls.
It has to be said that in comparison with the summer of 1944, when 205 Group was heavily engaged in operations against the Romanian oil industry, the last six months of the war for 205 Group saw relatively few casualties. There was often quite a lot of flak over industrial targets, most of these were railway marshalling yards - but not many searchlights and very few fighters, either by day or night. Most bombing operations, but not all, were carried out at night. Supply drops to the Yugoslav partisans were carried out sometimes by day, sometimes by night. I don't recall that we ever met any real opposition on these trips. The Russian advance had removed Romania from the target list and most raids were within Northern Italy, Austria and Yugoslavia. The weather conditions though were appalling and this accounted for some losses and abandoned operations, where containers would be brought back and some bomb loads, although jettisoning of bombs was common to ease the landing of the aircraft. Operating conditions, as distinct from domestic conditions, were fair to moderate. Tortorella had a runway surfaced with PSP - which I understand means pierced steel plank, 'though it is said there are other versions". The PSP was raised 9 inches above ground level and was like

Shadows of the Past

One of the Ploesti oil fields after a visit from Foggia-based squadrons, 1943/44.

giant pieces of meccano that linked together to make a sort of mat. The runway made a dreadful rattling noise whenever an aircraft moved on it and after rain, muddy water would squish up through the holes in it.

At one end of the runway was a shallow railway embankment, which didn't help in establishing a calm state of mind on take off. Aircraft were dispersed about the airfield in the usual way and crews taken in trucks to these when going on operations.

Nickels – Leaflets

'Nickels' was the name given to leaflets that were dropped in thousands over enemy occupied territories. They informed enemy personnel of various information. One in particular was a safe conduct pass, it read: the German soldier who carries this safe-conduct is using it as a sign of his genuine wish to give himself up. He is to be well looked after, to receive food and medical attention as required and is to be removed from the zone of combat as soon as possible.

The Nickels would arrive at the airfield in lorry loads and were distributed to the various aircraft and loaded near to the side flare chute for subsequent dropping. The wireless operator would usually be given the job of untying the bundles of leaflets and pushing them down the flare chute, which was first extended into the slipstream. If this was not carried out the nickels would be blown straight back into the aircraft.

Shadows of the Past

Three Wings

231 Wing with 37 and 70 Squadrons, 236 Wing with 40 and 104 Squadrons and 330 Wing with 142 and 150 Squadrons each operated the Wellington Mark X bomber through most of 1944 from their bases in Southern Italy. It had been withdrawn from Bomber Command and home-based squadrons the previous year as being no longer adequate for the job in the night skies over Germany. The aircraft though was much respected by the crews who flew them and the Wellington was known affectionately to them as the 'Wimpey'.

More Memories
Sergeant Bryney Watkins
37 Squadron
205 Group
Italy

July – December 1944

It all started at I.T.W.Hillside Bulawayo, Southern Rhodesia where after 2½ years on the staff, during which time I spent leaves at Victoria Falls Hotel, Salisbury, and many other places of interest. On many occasions, I visited the Hills of Matapas (Worlds Eye View). It is here that John Cecil Rhodes is buried, his grave being hewn out of solid rock. It is here that the Welsh Exiles met to have one large picnic on St.David's Day and in the evening held a dance in the Grand Hotel, Bulawayo.

As I said, it was 2½ years and feeling it was time for a change, I remustered to go on an Air Gunners course, after being accepted, I did part of the course here at I.T.W.Hillside. After passing my course, I went on to the Gunnery School, Moffat near Givelo on Ansons, using the old water-cooled Vickers guns. It was a hard struggle having had no secondary schooling, my parents just could not afford it, but I managed to squeeze through. It was now time for me to embark on my journey of a lifetime, which was to take me through Southern Rhodesia, Northern Rhodesia, Belgium Congo and over the lake Tangayisa which took 11 hours by paddle steamer then on to Kisumo on the edge of the lakes Victoria in Tanganyika itself. I spent a day here enjoying a swim in a part of the lake which had been meshed off, to keep the crocodiles out.

Shadows of the Past

The following day saw me flying by Loadstar aircraft over the Sudan and touching down at Khartoum to spend a pleasant evening in the faithful Sergeant's Mess, followed by a good nights sleep.

Next morning after breakfast, went to see the place where, Gordon was slain, and sat down on the very steps where he died. A little later I was back in the air leaving the Sudan behind and on over Egypt to touch down at main airfield. I spent a few days billeted in a Royal Palace.

I did not enjoy the same comforts as King Farouk as I had to sleep on the cold marble floor, but apart from this, it was quite an experience. The few days I spent in Egypt I visited many places of interest, the Pyramids, Museum and of course certain places of entertainment, belly dancers, the dance of the seven veils and several exhibitions, which was enlightening to a young inexperienced lad like me. All good things must end, so once again I was on my way by road to Palestine to do my O.T.U. For a few days, I was billeted in the Italian Hospital. It was so cold at night and to keep warm, one had to sleep in full flying kit including boots.

I never forget the night I arrived in Jerusalem there was barbed wire everywhere. Armoured vehicles were in the streets, this was because of the Jewish terrorist's storm gang led by Mr Begin, later to become Prime Minister of Israel. It was not safe to go out at night anywhere in Jerusalem. Many of the servicemen died by the hands of Jews, the very people we were fighting for in Europe.

On now to 77 OTU. At Gastineau Quastina near to Tel Aviv to join three other crews in "B", flight to train in Wellingtons. Out of the four crews in "B" flight, ours were the only crew to survive. Two crews on returning from cross-countries over Cairo and Alexandria, crashed near to the runway killing all the aircrew. I was one of the bearers at their burial at Ramlah Cemetery near Jerusalem. The other crew were scrubbed, Pilot unsuitable, both the aircraft that crashed we flew in on the previous nights on cross-countries. Half-way through the course we had a weeks leave in Jerusalem, during this time I was able to visit those places we have read about in the bible, namely Church of Nativity, Mount of Olives Garden of Gethsemane, Bethlehem, Wailing Wall, Dome on the Rock,

Shadows of the Past 130

River Jordon, Dead Sea, Sea of Galilee and a visit to Jericho. On the completion of the course, I spent a week's leave in Tel Aviv. It was there I met an old friend from Brynmawr, namely Cecil Ciddle, who was a Jew, he was on leave from Ismalia, and was an instrument mechanic in the R.A.F. Of course, we went to all the best places and it was all on the house. It was here I had my photograph taken with another Air Gunner, Jimmy Miller in Ben Kirken Street, the street of a thousand prostitutes. Jimmy went missing on his final op over Yugoslavia.

Once again, I was on the move by road back to Egypt and to Almagi transit camp just outside Cairo. It was here that I met Jonathan Brynmawr's lad, a W/O WOP Jack Williams who had done a tour during the desert campaign and now on his way to South Africa as an instructor. We met later back in Brynmawr had a few pints together and just after Jack went berserk, apart for a short spell he has been a patient in Tolgarth Mental Hospital.

Leaving Almasa transit camp, I was taken to the American airbase at Payne's Field just outside of Cairo to be flown over to Italy. While having a cup of coffee in the canteen I saw this group dressed in strange uniforms and being nosy, I asked them who they were. It turned out that they were the equivalent to our Ensa, and they were Andre Kastelanetz, his wife Lily Pons (The pocketsize Prim Ad Dona and the Orchestra. They were also on their way to Italy to entertain the troops. We chatted together until it was time for take off in one D63 and us in another. We flew down to North African coast over many of the battle zones – Benghazi, Tripoli, landing at Castle Benito for a M.V. lunch then over the Messina Straights to land at Naples Airfield

I must say what charming people the Americans were to talk to; they wanted to know all about us, where we were from in the United Kingdom. We parted at Naples; they wished us all the best and safe landing. Meeting them and talking to them was one of my happiest memories of the war. From Naples, it was transit time again, this time at Portici not far from Mount Vesuvius. I was here in 1944 when it erupted

Shadows of the Past 131

The new Liberator bombers arrive, Tortorella, 1944.

Typical Italian country scene.

Foggia

A smouldering Vasuvious.

70 Sqn Liberator, Foggia, 1945.

Shadows of the Past

They went again to visit many places out of the history books, Pompeii, Sorrento, Isle of Capri, Isle of Ischia, and Salerno Cassino. It was now time to join the Squadron, which was 37 at Tortorella near Foggia, Northern Italy. Our first trip was on the 7/8.8.1944, it was to be the airfield at Szombathely in Hungary, a good start, plenty of fighters, flak. No.2 was the marshalling yards at Kraljivo in Yugoslavia, plenty of enemy action. No.3 was again the airfield at Hadjie Baszonmany in Hungary, crawling with night fighters. No.4 was a raid on Marseilles the night before the Southern Italy invasion. As we returned over the sea, I could see from my turret the ships going in for the landing. No.5 was to be the Xenia Oil Refinery in Rumania but had to return early due to oxygen failure. Was put on close arrest when landing until oxygen bottles were checked, my bottle was empty, no lack of moral fibre.! No.6 – this was a spare trip, as my pilot Dicky Ockendon was grounded because of a nasty carbuncle on back of his neck, which had to be lanced. I did four spare Dicky trips. The crew I went with was F/O Reed Pilot, his navigator Sgt Bone, the rest of the crew was made up by F/Lt John Archer bombing leader, the wireless operator an Australian known as Shorty and yours truly. The target was the German Goring tank works in Austria. We took off at 19.40 hours; after being airborne for about 2 hours, the voice of the navigator came over the intercom telling us we were lost and saying how sorry he was. You can imagine what it was like. This is the patter that went on – Dicky - " Sorry Pilot",
Pilot – "too bloody late to be sorry, get us back on track"
Pilot to Bombing Leader - "what do you think we should do Sir", his reply "carry on regardless, Wireless Operator – "drop the bloody bombs and turn round". This went on for another hour, I was in the turret laughing my head off, I couldn't help it, it was funny, and it would be great for television.
Pilot to Wireless Operator "Throw some window out?", shortly in reply, "What do you think I have been doing this last hour?". Then the voice of the Navigator came over to say he had worked it out and gave the Pilot the reading, and by now, we were only a half hour late and as we approached the target area once again Pilot to Shorty - "Throw more windows out". Shorty "Its all bloody gone drop the bomb and turn back"
At last we reached the target, bombs away, there was no enemy action, they must have all gone home to bed as we were so late. After this episode, the Navigator was known as Sgt. Bonehead.

Shadows of the Past

No 7, this was again a spare Dicky trip with Sgt Reynolds Pilot, the target Szony Oil Refinery in Hungary, once again heavy enemy flak and fighters on our way back. Then the Bomb Aimer informed us that we had a 500 lb bomb hung up. Luckily for us, however, he got rid of it into the sea before crossing the Italian mainland. I was to go with the same crew the following night, their own gunner Sgt Kilner was grounded for sleeping in the turret two nights before. Another aircraft damaged part of the tail plane. I was on my way back to pick my gear up from the tent when the Wingco told me not to bother; their own gunner had learnt his lesson. There for the grace of god go I, they went but never returned even after identing.

No 8 again spare Dicky with Sgt Malcolm Jones the Marshalling Yards at Bologna, Northern Italy, plenty of flak.

No.9 back with own crew this was what we call a battle stooge, we were requested by the eighth army to do a low level bombing raid on the Gothic Line at Pesaro, where Field Marshall's troops were dug in, could not be moved (Kesselring). Our troops lit fires on their side of the line as markers. We went in at four hundred feet and all our bombs fell on the German line. Next day our army broke through, we had a thank you very much from our Commanders.

No.10 again a Marshalling Yard in Italy, this time Ferraro, very little enemy action.
No.11 the same target as No.10.
No.12 Marshalling yards - this time Ravenna, Italy.
No.13 as raids nos. 10 and 11.
No.14 A full moon, which meant mine laying, a trip up the Danube in Hungary, two mines at a thousand pounds each.

These raids we called the "splash raids" because we had to come down to below one hundred feet to drop the mines and when they entered the water, the splash came up over the aircraft, there was even water in my turret. Many of our aircraft were forced to ditch because of the heavy gunfire. Our aircraft seemed to be on fire because of the flaming onion they were throwing up at us. We seemed to be looking down the gun barrels.

Shadows of the Past

On pinpointing our section of the river, the mines were dropped and after much evasive action, we headed back to base and all the way back I could see aircraft that had crashed, up in flames like Guy Fawkes night. These were all pinpointed by our Navigator. Only once did I go on these drops and once was enough to last me a lifetime, it was flak all the way there and all the way back.

No 15 a change of scenery, this time a raid on the aerodrome of Eleusis near Athens, Greece. This was to prevent the Germans using the runways in their evacuation, not much enemy action, and light flak.
No 16 another battle stooge, bombing of troop concentrations around Rimini, Northern Italy, and some flak.
No 17 Hungary once again, this time the Marshalling Yards, Hessyeshalom. Much enemy action, fighters, heavy flak, there and back.

It was now time for a spot of rest leave, we travelled by road, some parts were very hair-raising, just as dangerous as flying. At last, we reach Sorrento and it was here in the Minerva Hotel we were to spend a week to recuperate. Again, I was to visit most of the tourist attractions as I did whilst in transit in Poritici earlier.

Leave over, we returned to Tortorella to continue our tour of ops: -
No 18 a change of venue this time, it was to be a bridge near St Benedetti, Italy – a quiet trip.
No 19 this time it was to be a Viaduct at Borovnica in Yugoslavia, some fighters, much flak.
No 20 this was a most interesting raid – the Marshalling Yards at Verona. We did not have a chance to say hello to Romeo and Juliet, we were too busy with the Germans.
No 21 back once again to Hungary, the Marshalling Yards at Szekesfeneryar. On this raid, we carried the four thousand cookie and by god were we happy to hear these words "Bombs gone", much flak, fighters.
No 22 this time the yards at Zagreb, East Yugoslavia, not too much enemy action.
No 23 once again to Hungary the Zombatheley Aerodrome, as before heavy flak and fighters.

Shadows of the Past

No 24 something different for a change, a daylight supply drop to the Yugoslavian Partisans up in the mountains. I could see the white V marked on the ground, surrounded by waving partisans.

No 25 as No.24

No 26 as No.24

No 27 as No.24

No 28 bombing raid on Marshalling Yards, Sarajevo, Yugoslavia. Slight enemy action on the way back to base. One of our aircraft was right behind and the Pilot a French Canadian F/O Lavack was giving me the old V sign up-you-Jack, I replied up-you-too. He tried to beat us back to join the circuit, but anyway we landed first. We were halfway down the runway, my turret turned to starboard when all of a sudden there was this bloody big bang. Dick my Pilot came over the intercom "Bryn what's that", I replied "its okay here", but on turning the turret astern I could see this other Wellington not far behind us up in flames. It was the aircraft of the French Canadian, they had landed with a bomb aboard. Instead of usual crew of five there were six, and the Pilot walked away unharmed, but the rest of the crew were killed. There were so many bits and pieces covering the runway that the aircraft that were still in the air, were diverted to other airfields. Unknowing to my Pilot Dick, his cousin an Army Officer was waiting for us in dispersal. He was on leave from the Front and someone had told him that it was our plane that had blown up and when we got out of the aircraft he saw Dick and put his arms around him and started to cry like a baby, he was so glad to see him alive.

No 29 Now this was the worst of all. It was to be a supply drop to the Italian Partisans near Genoa. The day started with heavy rain, thunder and lightning, there was no changes come dinnertime and we were all sure it would be scrubbed, but no, it was still on and the weather was the worst I have experienced.

Time for briefing, it was still very bad weather with low cloud, rain, thunder lightning and strong winds – the lot.

We took off at 17.56 hrs, but were unable to climb more than a few thousand feet because of the low cloud and the only way over the sea was through the cloud. A break in the Manfrederici Mountains marked by a white flashing beacon. We set course, but it was not long before we

Shadows of the Past

*Containers dropping in Slovenia, 1945.
Photos: Museum of Contemporary History, Ljubljana.*

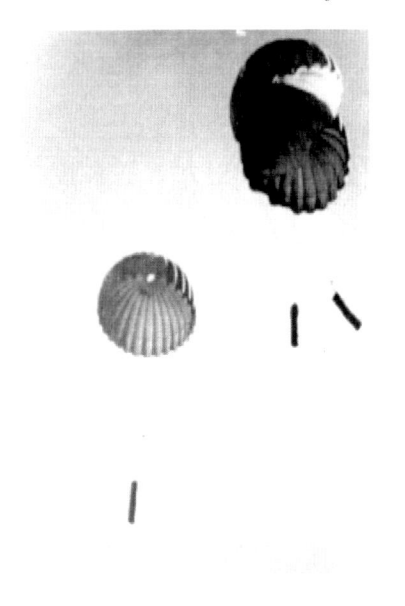

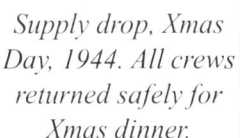

Supply drop, Xmas Day, 1944. All crews returned safely for Xmas dinner.

could see it was impossible and the compass packed up because of the conditions. We were lost after about an hour, the Wireless Operator tried to call Darkie for a fix, but no joy, we were dropping as much as five hundred feet. All round the aircraft was a halo of static and there seemed to be lights like electric bulbs on the end of my four guns also we were so low I could see the white horses on the rough sea. I though – Oh God, this is it, a grave in the angry sea. The Pilot decided to abandon this mad, stupid venture and told us to look out for the beacon. I spotted it on our starboard beam and called up the Pilot to tell him, straight away we headed for it back over the mainland. Then we could not find our airfield at Tortorella, we had to land at Foggia Main. The outcome of this bloody escapade was that we lost thirty aircraft, Wellingtons and Liberators out of a force of one hundred, all because of bad weather. One of our crews, the Pilot being W/O Jeremy Pike, were on their 70th op, they crashed in the hills near to our airfield and they all died of exposure, six aircraft got through to drop supplies.

The Sorrento coast, & view from the Minerva Hotel, 1944, where most crews spent some leave.

In my logbook, it says, "Returned early, bad weather 2 hrs 35 mins. What a waste of good aircrew and aircraft. Lest we forget – I shall never".

No.30 this was a repeat of No.29 but in good weather. We all got to the dropping point and all got back safe, supplies were dropped on target.
No.31 a raid on the bridge and troops at Podgorica, Yugoslavia, some flak.
No.32 another raid in Yugoslavia, the town of Visegrad, roads and troops as the Germans were retreating. Flak.
No.33 Yugoslavia once again, the town of Uzice and troops. There were many thousands of Germans in and around the town. There were heavy casualties amongst the enemy.
No.34 again a supplies drop to the Yugoslavian Partisans near Tuzla, up in the mountains. This was our last trip and after we dropped, our supplies out Pilot flew very low in salute to the Partisans who were waving to us.

Shadows of the Past

I threw them the small tin of boiled sweets we had in our iron rations. I have often wondered if they enjoyed those sweets.

My assessments read so, above average, a good hard working Air Gunner, keen and reliable, should make a useful instructor. H A Langton W/Cdr now known as Sir Henry Calley D.S.O. D.F.C. (This was not too bad for a lad who just managed to scrape through in Rhodesia.)

Supply drop, Circhina, January 18th, 1945.

I spent Christmas 1944 with the lads at Tortorello, then back on the road once again to Portici. In transit I met two more boys from Brynmawr, one was an airman the other a sailor, Jack Thomas and Tom Vaughan. They were both on the Isle of Ischia and I spent a weekend with them, very nice it was too, living with an Italian family, mama was very kind to us. All good things come to an end and I was on my way by train to Taranto, which took 15 hrs, what a nightmare. There were no lights and no heating and on top of this I had one of my kitbags stolen, it happened to be the one with all my flying kit and souvenirs in. Then by American

*Shirts being made from parachutes, Paka, NE Slovenie, July 1944.
Photo: Museum of Contemporary History, Ljubljana.*

Shadows of the Past

Liberty boat to Egypt back to Almaza. The Americans were great to us on the boat over kindness itself. What a contrast to the way we were treated on the awful boat Empress of Scotland one of our own. They treated us like dogs and we were ordered to do gun watches, then straight after, boat drill. We had no sleep and we were begrudged a cup of tea after being on watch for hours. We were on this 'bloody' boat for six weeks, calling in at Algeria, Gibraltar and Malta and not being allowed to set foot on land – so much for our wonderful Merchant Navy.

We disembarked at Liverpool and as we stood on the quay, we told these kind sailors what we should like to see happen to their lousy boat. Then on to West Kirby to be kitted out and given ration cards and pay, then a nice warm meal of sausages and potatoes (the best meal for seven weeks).

After good nights sleep, it was time to catch the train for South Wales. I arrived in Newport station just on midnight; the last train had gone up the valley, so after over three years abroad I was so near and yet so far away from home. I thought to myself, it's a night in the Chapel on Stow hill for me, but suddenly a voice came over the tannoy asking passengers for the Western Valley to go to the Station Master's office. When I got there, it was full of sailors, soldiers, and airmen. One of the soldiers was a boy Addis, whom I knew. The Station Master told us he would put on a train as far as Aberbeeg, God Bless Him. When we got to Aberbeeg, apart from us two Brynmawr boys, the train was empty. We got off the train and were about to walk away, when the driver asked us how far we had to go, we told him Brynmawr, he said jump back on I will take you there – what a wonderful gesture after the way I was treated on that terrible boat. I shall always remember this driver, bless him, he made up for those on that boat.

We got to Brynmawr just after one o'clock, the station was all in darkness and locked up, and so we had to climb over the fence. As I had a suitcase and three kit bags I decided to leave two kitbags on the station and before I got up the following morning, my bags were brought up to our house by Mr Edgar Simmons the drayman. On arriving back home in Clydach Street, I found the street full of flags and all the neighbours and my family waiting for me, what a homecoming. I had tears of joy and felt like the Prodigal Son. Here I was, back in my hometown after three years of travel from the Clyde to Durban, then from Durban to Cairo, from Cairo to Tottorello, Italy and from here to fly over seven European countries, to me it was a journey of a lifetime.

Now to end I must tell you a story; when I look back upon it, I have had many a laugh, but it could have had serious bearings on my RAF career.

One morning not long after returning from a raid, I was trying to get some sleep, which was not always easy when the blankets are damp and your bed is a lid off a packing case. I heard someone asking for Bryn Watkins and there in the opening of the tent stood this soldier, he came in and then I could see he was a Brynmawr boy named Jack Williams. I asked him how did he find me and he replied that he had met another Brynmawr boy, Jack Cable in Foggia who told him about me. I then asked him what he was doing and he replied that he was on leave from the front and that he was in the same mob as a cousin of mine, namely Gareth Davies who won the Military Medal, but died of his wounds a couple of years ago.

He had nothing with him, only what he stood up in, so I gave him spare battle blouse to wear with stripes, he then came to have a meal with me in the Sgt's Mess and I gave him a few lire to have a drink of wine in our farmhouse converted mess. When the week was up, he asked could he have a look inside an aircraft, as he had never been in a plane, so I showed him over a Wellington. We then started to walk along the side of the runway and I could see this Wellington up on an air test, there was no other aircraft about. As the Wellington came into land she seemed to wobble; we continued further up the runway, the aircraft wings started to flap and I could see she was going to crash. I grabbed my friend and pulled him down into a slit trench. When the plane crashed it came down about fifty feet from the bomb dump and apart from the rear gunner, who was dragged from the turret, the rest of the crew were burnt alive. As you may know, normally on an air test, it is the Pilot and one other, who sit in the turret who go, but this was a new crew, straight from O.T.U. who were all keen to fly. It was now time for Jack Williams to return to his unit, so he told me; I loaded him up with Cigs, as they were plentiful, razor blades and soap and asked him to share them with my cousin. On meeting my cousin some time later in Brynmawr, I asked him, did he enjoy the Cigs etc., which I had sent him via Jack Williams, he laughed, explaining to me that Jack had been a deserter and he had been on the run all the time he was with me. I have not seen him since.

Comrades, every word I have written is the truth, the whole truth, nothing but the truth, so help me God. In my logbook, I have the dates and times of all my ops, but the stories are in my mind forever. Note: -

In recognition of the part I played in the liberation of Yugoslavia, I am a member of the British Yugoslav Society; this is to continue the close comradeship that had been built up during the war years.

My wife Rose and I have been honoured guests of the Ambassador and his wife at their Embassy in London on many occasions and have been treated as V.I.P.

In recognition of my 34 ops over seven European countries, I received only the Italian Star, but did not get the Aircrew Europe Star because I did not start my tour until after the 5th of June 1944 – what a load of rubbish. Many hundreds of Aircrew were killed after this date, fighting the same war and some did a lot more than those who received the award.

Tortorella, Italy: No 37 Squadron

December 1st, 1944
Operations, nothing to report. No operations due to bad weather.

Liberators aircraft are now arriving for conversion, but once more plans are changed. This time the decision being to operate the aircraft with crews ready trained, to be posted forthwith.

Note: All 37 flight crews to transfer to 70 Sqn as Liberator crews became available.
Discipline - stray dogs have become rather numerous on the domestic campsites, although quite a number have already been destroyed in accordance with notices published in D.R.O.'s to this effect.

Shadows of the Past

Bad Weather Notices
November 25th: Due to the very bad weather across Italy and the Balkans, no more operations were carried out during November.
Note : The weather was appalling for this part of Europe. Snow fell on the Foggia Plain which was most unusual. Snow had not been seen to fall in living memory.

November 11th, 1944: Court of Enquiry; Squadron Leader Hubbard, Flight Lieutenant Fitzimmons and Flying Officer McGowen of 70 Squadron conducted a Court of Enquiry into the circumstances of aircraft LP 603 which had blown up on November 7th.

First Operation, Italian Tour
37 Squadron, 'B' Flight, No 205 Group, Tortorella (Foggia)

October 18[th,] 1944
After settling in at Tortorella and getting to know where everything was, Tubby was flying Wellingtons X LP329 with Flying Officer Jay and Flight Sergeant Navern for airframe and engine test and to familiarise himself with the surrounding countryside. The flight was uneventful and flying time was 48 minutes.

October 20th/21st, 1944
First Operation, bombing Zsombathley Aerodrome, Hungary.
It was two days later, October 20th; Tubby was to fly his first operation as 2nd pilot with a crew that was unknown to him. The target was an aerodrome at Zsombathley, Hungary. The crew was: -

Wellington LP259
F/O LAVACK: 1st pilot
W/O GAUNT: 2nd pilot
Sgt TREWICK: navigator
W/O WHITE: bomb aimer
W/O STANFORD: wireless op
F/SGT DONLERCY: rear gunner
Up 1850, down 0018 hrs.

37 Sqn crest.

Shadows of the Past

Details of Sortie: -
The trip was five hours 28 minutes long. The bomb load consisted of 9 x 500 lb GP and Nickels. Two of 37 Squadron's aircraft missing.

The operation went without any problems, the target was found and bombed, and bombs were seen to hit the airfield. 74 aircraft took off from Group, five failed to return (3.7%).

All new pilots were crewed with experienced skippers to get to know the ropes and generally familiarise themselves with the procedure of operations.

Summary of Events
Weather was good but hazy at target area.

16 aircraft were airborne. 'T' (Warrant Officer Robson) was missing. The remainder attacked dropping 2 x 4,000 lb HE, 2 x 2,000 lb HE, 109 x 500 lb HE and 65 packets of leaflets, 1 from 9,000/7,000 feet at 2101 – 2202 hrs. Illumination was on time and well placed but target markers were three - four minutes late and several crews made second runs. Difficulty was experienced in pinpointing T.I's due to haze and dying illumination but reports indicate that they fell near the two aiming points. No fighter interception. Buildings and two hangers received direct hits, one Me 110 destroyed. The runway well pitted with bomb craters.

Conversion to Heavy Bomber Status
Two Liberators Mark VI aircraft delivered for Squadron conversion.

Second Operation: Supply Dropping, Jugoslavia: Operation TOFFEE

October 31st was to see Tubby as 2nd pilot again with another crew, of whom he knew little. The operation was supply dropping to the partisan's forces in Tuzla, Yugoslavia, who were harassing the retreat of the German forces from that country. Yugoslavia was the only country during the war that freed itself; pushing the Germans out with the help of the RAF and USAF. It would be interesting to know how much help each provided. Overall, it could have been 50-50, but it may well have been 80% British help, with Americans providing 20% of total help provided, it was mainly

Shadows of the Past

squadrons from 205 Group, who bombed bridges, roads, troop concentrations and supplied food, arms and medical aid.

Wellington LP575

W/O SHIEL:	1st pilot
W/O GAUNT:	2nd pilot
Sgt GOLDSBOROUGH:	navigator
Sgt PITTOCK:	air gunner & bomb aimer
Sgt MAITLAND:	wireless operator
Sgt HOUGHTON:	rear gunner

Up 1411 hrs, down 1756 hrs.

Details of Sortie
The ground signal was seen and six J2 containers dropped. Town seen, all chutes seen to open. 11 packets of nickels dropped on SM/R (60 aircraft took part, no losses reported. Flying time three hours 45 minutes). No casualties.

Summary of Events
14 aircraft operated and dropped 81 containers from 4,000 – 5,500 feet. Sky markers were dropped and 11 aircraft released their containers on them, the remainder dropping visually on 'E' signal or on fire (beacon). 170 packets of leaflets were dropped east and the target area. Weather cloudy on route but mainly clear at target area. Opposition – slight inaccurate heavy and light flak from Mostar area.

Third Operation: (Tubby's first operation as 1st Pilot) Supply Dropping, Jugoslavia Sinj, Operation RELATOR

The very next day, November 1st, Tubby went to the briefing, pilots from 70 Squadron were coming out as they also used the same briefing hut, the orders were supply dropping in Yugoslavia again. The crew was part made up using RCAF volunteers. Sergeant Golsby Smith and Flight Sergeant Foster. Tubby was at least a little happier flying with his crew whom he knew personally and the two Canadians he had chosen.

November 1st, 1944

Wellington LP329

W/O GAUNT:	pilot
Sgt SCANLON:	navigator
Sgt SANDALL:	air gunner & bomb aimer
Sgt GOLSBY-SMITH (RCAF):	wireless operator
F/Sgt FOSTER (RCAF):	rear gunner

Up 1406 hrs, down 1725 hrs.

Details of Sortie
72 aircraft took part, no losses. Tubby's logbook indicated supply dropping six containers and nickels. Flying time three hours 20 minutes (one hold up). The release mechanism was frozen and the ground crew had to chop the container out when they landed.

Sergeant Bob Foster RCAF recalls that 'I had been posted to Foggia to replace lost A/C crews, that most unfortunate of situations - a "spare bod", and crews who had completed their tours'. Bob recalls his first meeting with Tubby, after volunteering to fill the vacant rear gunner's position. He had earlier spoken about volunteering for this operation to his own crew, who thought he was quite mad, as this operation would not count towards his own tour of duty with his present crew. He had made some enquiries about Tubby to the effect that he had already completed his first tour on Hampdens, so Bob had no reservations about going with a mature, experienced pilot. When Bob reported to Tubby for briefing, he found Tubby to be a very dapper and professional RAF man, who directed all the right questions at him (i.e. was he conversant with the weapons he was to use and the fighter tactics that were to be carried out). After a brief but condensed conversation, Tubby excused Bob, who went away to prepare himself for the afternoon operation feeling very confident.

The aircraft was taxied for take off and the crew went through the usual pre-flight checks. Take off went as planned. Bob thought that there was too much chitchat between the crew and remained quite alert to any situation. Approaching the drop zone the ground signal was seen and

Shadows of the Past

the containers dropped, but the bomb aimer reported a hold up. Only five containers dropped, whose chutes were all seen to open. After trying the release mechanism again and again, Tubby could do nothing else but return with the reluctant container. Bob was asked by Tubby if everything was OK as Bob had been very quiet during the trip. Bob answered, "Yes skipper". The aircraft touched down and taxied to a halt, to the biggest cheer from the crew. Bob asked why all the excitement, the bomb aimer, Maurice Sandell, answered that was our first operation with Tubby as first pilot. When Bob told his crew about the events with the "experienced" crew, they fell about with laughter.

Summary of Events

15 aircraft operated and dropped 90 containers of supplies and 173 packets of nickels. At 1510-1610 hrs from 700 - 1000 feet at a point between the town of Sinj, north of Split and a lake on the east side. A few crews saw the pre-arranged ground signal and containers were well concentrated in the correct area. Visibility was good and crews saw the ground swarming with the local inhabitants engaged in flag waving processions picking up the containers. There was no ground or air opposition.

Squadron News

Shower baths have been completed and are now working a roster of times for all ranks has been drawn up to avoid overcrowding.

Fourth Operation: Supply Dropping, Jugoslavia, Sanskimost Operation BALLINGCLAY

November 4th, 1944

Wellington XPLN914

W/O GAUNT:	pilot
Sgt SCANLON:	navigator
Sgt MCMELLIN:	wireless operator
Sgt HAZELDEN:	rear gunner
Sgt RIDING:	front gunner

Shadows of the Past

(The first sortie on which flew all of Tubby's crew).
Up 1317 hrs, down 16230 hrs

Details of Sortie
Five x 'E' containers and 12 packets of nickels dropped on chutes seen in target area, chutes seen to open ok. One container hung up brought back, no casualties.

Summary of Events
12 aircraft operated and dropped 71 containers at 1443-1452 from 550 - 900 feet near Sanskimost. All crews saw the town and dropped a good concentration on the ground signal. Weather was good and only slight inaccurate light flak was experienced. 144 packets of leaflets were dropped.

Aircraft operated from Group 92, no losses reported.

Fifth Operation: Supply Dropping Jugoslavia, Pregrad Operation FLOTSAM

November 5th, 1944

Wellington XT LP329
W/O GAUNT: pilot
Sgt GALL: front gunner
Sgt SCANLON: navigator
Sgt McMELLIN: wireless operator
Sgt SANDELL: air gunner & bomb aimer
Up 1143 hrs, down 1535 hrs.

Details of Sortie
Six x B containers and six packets of leaflets dropped on ground signal 'X'. One chute not seen to open. No casualties.

Summary of Events
11 aircraft operated and dropped 66 containers between 3129-1438 hrs from 500 - 900 feet near Pregrad (50 miles south west of Zagreb). All crews saw the dropping point marked with white strips and a good concentration of supplies reported. Weather good, no opposition. 78 packets of leaflets dropped en-route over Yugoslavia.

Shadows of the Past 149

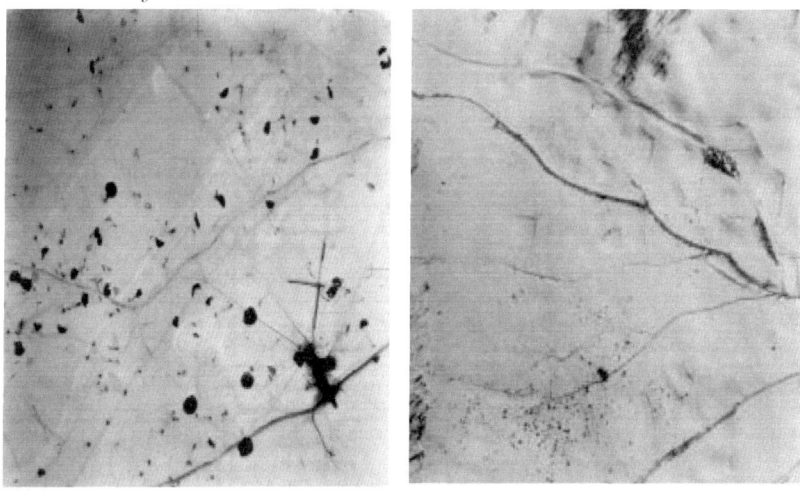

*Above: Supply drops, Flotsam area, February 2nd, 3rd & 7th, 1944.
All photos this page: Norman Moseley.*

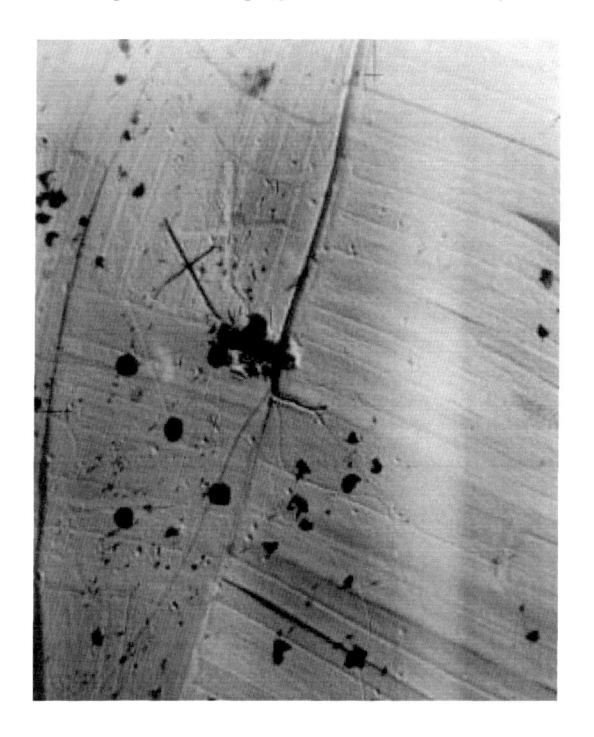

Sixth Operation: Supply Dropping, Pecora, Northern Italy
Operation PIRATE

November 12th, 1944

Wellington XA LN234
Sgt GAUNT: pilot
Sgt SCANLAN: navigator
Sgt MCMELLIN: wireless operator
Sgt SANDELL: air gunner & bomb aimer
Sgt HAZELDEN: rear gunner
Up 0632 hrs, Down 1320 hrs.

Details of Sortie
Six x '4' containers and 10 packets of nickels dropped on 'L' ground signal, chutes away ok. No casualties.

Summary of Events
10 aircraft were airborne but two returned early, one could not break cloud and the other had hydraulic trouble in the rear turret. Seven a/c saw the 'L' signal on the ground and dropped containers on this. One A/C did not see the 'L' so he did a DR (dead reckoning), dropping the containers at the end of the run. 10 containers hung up on various a/c, one returning with a full load. Containers dropped from 1105/1131 from 8,600 feet to 11,000 feet. Nickels dropped. Weather good. Opposition slight accurate heavy flak from battle area. Nil at T/A.

November 14th, 1944: Operations
The aircraft missing on 10th November was found crashed into the Gargan Mountains. The bodies of the crew were taken to No 336 wing sick quarters – later collected and coffined ready for burial.

November 15th, 1944: Operations
On approaching the runway aircraft LN789, piloted by Sergeant Duncan and crew, became uncontrollable on landing and crashed into the dispersal area. The bomb aimer walked out of the flaming wreckage and the rear gunner, Sergeant Foster, finding himself trapped in his turret, fought his way through the clear vision panel until he was about half way out of the a/c. At this stage he became trapped and went unconscious, but was rescued by two airmen who were on the scene very quickly.

Shadows of the Past
Sergeant 'Geordie' Hazelden Remembers

'The operation (November 4th) was supply dropping to Tito's partisans, as were the next two operations on 5th and 12th November. These operations were almost uneventful each time. The canisters with their food, guns, ammunition and medical supplies were dropped in daylight from 3-4,000 feet, usually 6,000 feet. It was not uncommon under small arms fire while flying down the valleys, the shooting coming straight across and sometimes coming down at you. On one side of the valley the enemy would be shooting at you, on the other side friendly forces would be waiting for the supplies'.

The number of aircraft in the November 4th operation were 92 no losses reported, November 5th night drop 93 aircraft no losses, and November 12th, 55 aircraft no losses. Riding came along on this trip as front gunner for extra defence in case of enemy fighter attack.

November 1944 saw almost a third of operations by 205 group supply dropping to Tito's partisans, the remaining operations were against the retreating German army, who were moving north out of Italy and Yugoslavia. The main targets were road and rail bridges marshalling yards and troop concentrations.

Seventh Operation: Bombing Troops & M/T, Sjenica

November 18th, 1944

Wellington MF471
Sgt GAUNT: pilot
Sgt SCANLON: navigator
Sgt McMELLIN: wireless operator
F/L COOK: bomb aimer
Sgt HAZELDEN: rear gunner
W/O WOODARD: front gunner
Up 1258 hrs, down 1626 hrs.

Shadows of the Past

Details of Sortie
Six x 500 lb GPNI 44, 12 x 250 lb GPNI, 44 packets of nickels dropped on motor transport north west of Sjenica. 7 trucks claimed. No casualties. Bombs dropped in three sticks.

Summary of Events
All attacked M/T and upwards of 30 vehicles (many of which left burning) were claimed. One vehicle was seen to blow up. Many thousands of rounds were fired by aircraft, no results seen. On this raid, Tubby went around the target area three times dropping a number of bombs on each pass.)

Eigth Operation: Bombing Troops & M/T, Sjenica - Pribj

November 19th, 1944

Wellington MF471
Sgt GAUNT: pilot
Sgt SCANLON: navigator
Sgt McMELLIN: wireless operator
Sgt SANDELL: bomb aimer
Sgt BARBEN: front gunner
Sgt HAZELDEN: rear gunner
Up 0930 hrs, down 1255 hrs.

Details of Sortie
Six x 500 lb GPNI, 12 x 250 lb GPNI and 15 packets of nickels dropped on M/T and buildings east of Karavda. Six trucks claimed destroyed.

Summary of Events
10 aircraft were once again operating to attack enemy motor transport and troops, moving out of Greece and Albania. The town of Sjenica and the roads north-west were identified. Good concentrations of M.T being found between Sjenica and Prije-Polje. Again, upwards of 30 vehicles claimed as destroyed (left burning). Many aircraft fired between 500 and 3500 rounds but no results observed. The aircraft bombed between 1113-1137 hrs from heights 5,000 feet to 9,800 feet at 1122 hrs and aircraft was seen on fire and a concentration of medium flak was observed in the Prije-Polje area. 1141 hrs aircraft, believed to be a Wellington, was seen burning on the ground.

Shadows of the Past 153

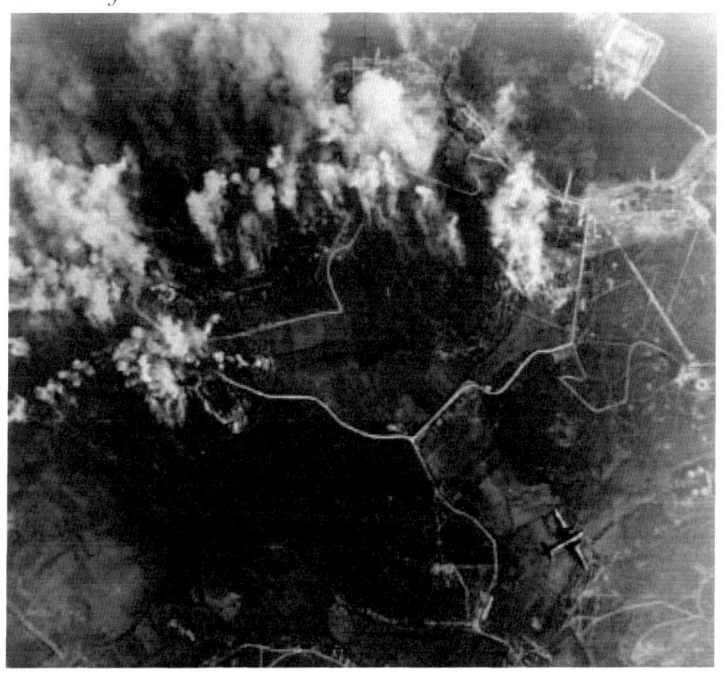

*Bombing Pola, February 21st, 1945.
Photo: Doug Skinner.*

Bombing Pola naval dockyards, March 3rd, 1945.

Shadows of the Past 154

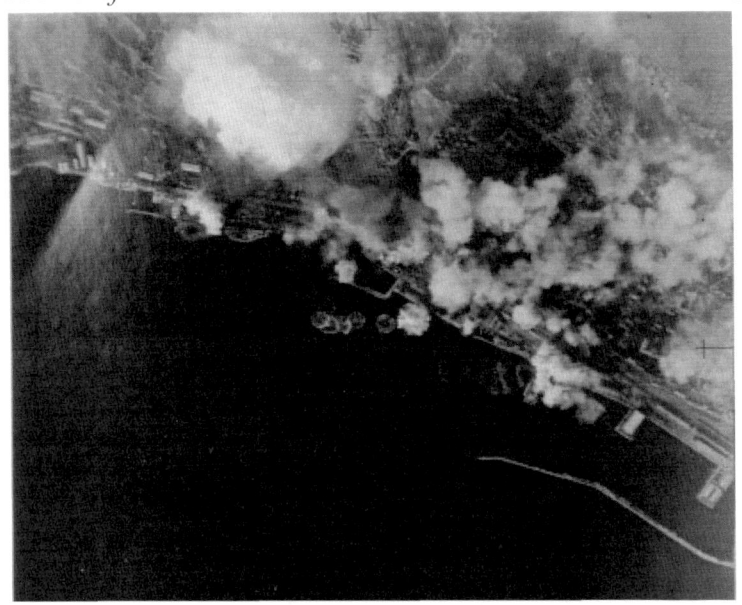

Bombing Fiume (Rieka) docks, February 15th, 1945.

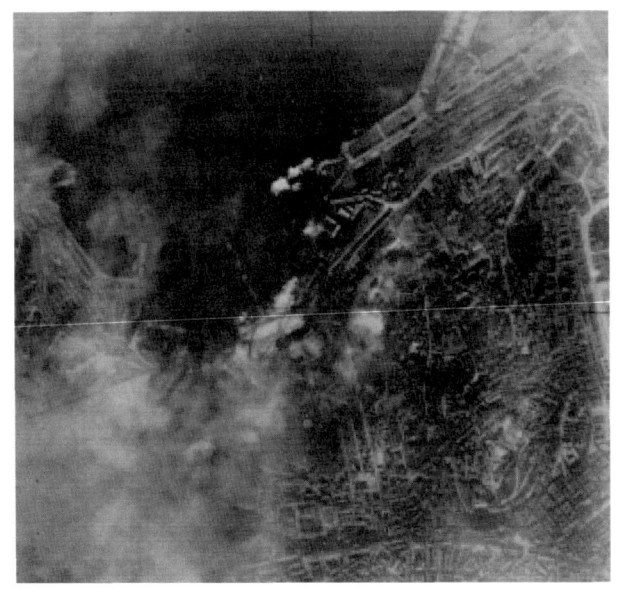

Target photo: Triest, February 17th, 1945.
Photo: Alan Isaac.

Shadows of the Past

Ninth Operation: Attack Troops & M/T, Visegrad –Prije - Polje

November 20th, 1944

Wellington MF471
Sgt GAUNT: pilot
Sgt SCANLON: navigator
Sgt McMELLIN: wireless operator
Sgt SANDELL: bomb aimer
W/O WOODARD: front gunner
Sgt HAZELDEN: rear gunner
Up 1340 hrs, down 1718 hrs.

Details of Sortie
12 x 250 lb GPNI 44, six x 500 lb GPNI and 13 packets of nickels dropped on M/T between Priboj and Prijepolje. Seven near missesclaimed, smoke seen. No casualties.

Summary of Events
Detailed to attack M/T and troop concentrations Visegrad Prije-Polje. 12 aircraft airborne and attacked, dropping 140 x 250 lb GPNI and 72 x 500 lb GPNI and 150 packets of nickels. T/A was identified by the town which itself was avoided. Direct hits on 12 MT were claimed and in addition, there were five claims of damaged roads. The main area coming under attack being between Dobran and a point half way between Kalafatovili and Prije-Polje. Roads were seen blocked at Ustobar and a landslide south of Priboj. Bombing took place 1512 - 1544 hrs from 6,500 to 10,000 feet. Weather good.

Tenth Operation: Bombing Troop Concentration, Uzice Town

November 23rd, 1944

Wellington LP329
Sgt GAUNT: pilot
Sgt McMELLIN: wireless operator
Sgt SANDELL: bomb aimer
Sgt HAZELDEN: rear gunner

Shadows of the Past

Sgt SCANLON: navigator
Up 1310 hrs, down 1638 hrs.

Details of Sortie
Six x 500 lb GPTI, 12 x 250 lb GPNI and 10 packets of nickels dropped on town. No results observed. Observed concentration, dust and smoke and fire at north end of target area. Aircraft sustained minor flak holes on aileron and fuselage in target area.

Summary of Events
10 A/c were airborne for this operation. 'D' (Flight Sergeant Brookfield) failed to return. 47 x 500 lb 6PTI; 94 x 250 GPTI; 1 x 4000 lb and 90 pkts of leaflets were dropped from 1,000 to 10,000 ft at 1600/1504 hours. Target was identified firstly by yellow TIs and subsequently by the amount of smoke and dust rising from the town, where a good concentration of bomb bursts were seen. At 1601 two large explosions in the T/A were followed by two pillars of thick black smoke. 'V' (Flying Officer Lavack) was hit just after dropping his bombs and received damage to starboard wing, engine and fuselage, bombing panel was also holed slightly. Captain Mann, the navigator, was wounded by shrapnel and was detained in hospital on return. 'T' (W/O Gaunt) received two minor holes in aileron.

Weather - patches of stratus heavy and slight over Adriatic. T/A clear and visibility good.
Opposition - Moderate accurate heavy and slight inaccurate light flak from target, moderate accurate heavy from Visegrad and from the roads to the west of T/A near Dobran there was slight inaccurate heavy and light encountered.

Eleventh Operation: Supply Dropping, Jugoslavia
Detailed Supply Dropping, Bugojno, Jugoslavia
Operation BALLINCLAY

November 25th, 1944

Wellington MF471
Sgt GAUNT: pilot
Sgt SCANLON: navigator

Shadows of the Past

Sgt McMELLIN: wireless operator
Sgt SANDELL: bomb aimer
Sgt HAZELDEN: rear gunner
W/O WOODWARD: front gunner
Up 1203 hrs, down 1505 hrs

Details of Sortie
Six x 'D' containers, 12 pkts Nickels dropped on red sky markers. No casualties.

Summary of Events
Eight aircraft were airborne and dropped 47 'D' type containers. One aircraft bringing one container back due to hang up. The target was identified by red sky markers, checked by 'Gee" (The Radar System). There was no opportunity for a visual check due to cloud. A good concentration of chutes were observed, although aircraft seen to drop on various headings, probably due to the lateness of the sky markers. Spitfires were flown as cover. Weather 10/10 clouds en route. S/C with tops at 7,000 feet falling off to 9/10 at target area. No opposition.

November 24th, 1944
The previous day, Flying Officer Cave had starboard wing holed by containers falling from another aircraft, but returned safely to base.

Sport
The Squadron 1st Xl Football Team drew 0-0 with No. 240 Wing in the 205 Group Football League.

Accident
A M/T accident occurred on the main road leading from the campsite to Foggia, near the camp, in which Lance Corporal Morgan, the driver of one of the lorries in the collision was injured and the lorry was slightly damaged.

Twelfth Operation: Bombing Troop Concentrations, Podgorica

December 3rd, 1944

Wellington X 'W' LP 674
Sgt GAUNT: pilot
Sgt SCANLON: navigator
Sgt SANDELL: bomb aimer
Sgt McMELLIN: wireless operator
Sgt HAZELDEN: rear gunner
W/O WOODARD:
Up 1302 hrs, down 1607 hrs

Details of Sortie
Six x 500 GP, 12 x 250 GP, Nickels, eight packets. .

No ground detail in T/A visible due to 10/10 cloud. Eight packets nickels dropped – all bombs jettisoned in Adriatic. No casualties.

Summary of Events
Detailed to attack troop concentrations in Podgorica - Klopot. Seven Wellingtons and two Liberators took off on this operation. 'Q' (Pilot Officer Morgan) had to return very early due to port engine trouble and had to jettison his load in the fields four miles east of Foggia. The aircraft had to make a 'belly' landing on reaching base, but all the crew was uninjured. Of the remaining nine aircraft (including the two Liberators), were unable to find the target area owing to cloud cover 10/10 and jettisoned bombs in Adriatic.

'P' (Flight Sergeant Barratt) descended through the cloud and attacked concentrations of MT and troops stationary alongside the roadside, north and south of Boicle. The other two aircraft attacked from 9,000 feet through gaps in the cloud cover. One aircraft claimed two hits on two roads. 30 x 250 GPM and 63 pkts of Nickels were dropped altogether.

All aircraft returned - no casualties.

Thirteenth Operation: Supply Dropping, Tuzla, Jugoslavia
Operation TOFFEE
December 4th, 1944

Wellington X 'P' LP 646
Sgt GAUNT: pilot
Sgt SCANLON: navigator
Sgt McMELLIN: wireless operator
Sgt SANDELL: bomb aimer
W/O WOODARD: front gunner
Sgt HAZELDEN :   rear gunner
Up 1256 hrs, down 1650 hrs.

70 Sqn crest.

Details of Sortie
Six x 'S' Containers 12 Pkts Nickels - Dropped on 'A' (+ 1 small fire) - No casualties.

Summary of Events
Detailed for supply dropping Tuzla. 10 aircraft, including two Liberators were detailed for this supply-dropping sortie. 'A' (Flying Officer Buhr) had to return early due to engine trouble. The remainder carried 19 x 'WS' and 47 'WD' containers and 95 packets nickels. Encountered only 5/10 medium cloud, base 13,000 feet, en route, clear target area and good visibility.

Details of Sortie
T/A was easily identified, the early arrivals dropping their containers on 'A' in white canopies. The remainder unable to identify the 'A' because of the concentration of chutes on the ground. Dropped on 'G' fixes ground signals and 'Verey' signals. Opposition moderate, heavy flak from Sarajevo, slight heavy flak from Mostar and slight inaccurate light flak from Jablanca - Kosvjic. All aircraft returned safely.

Shadows of the Past
Fourteenth Operation: Bombing Troops & M/T, Matesevo - Kolasin

December 19th, 1944

Wellington X 'H' MF367
W/O GAUNT: pilot
Sgt SCANLAN: navigator
Sgt SANDELL: bomb aimer
Sgt McMELLIN: wireless operator
Sgt HAZELDEN: rear gunner
Up 1311 hrs, Down 1547 hrs.

Details of Sortie
6 x 500 GP 12 x 250 GP Nickels.

Road MT seen and bombs dropped in 3 sticks from 3,000 feet aimed at roads, bombs seen to straddle the road.

Detailed to Bomb MT and Troops (concentrations on road) Matesevo – Kolasin.

Summary of Events
11 aircraft took off to continue yesterday's work. One returned early with engine trouble, and the remainder found the target. Area clear of cloud as on previous days and smote the Hun heavily. There were many hits on the road and several fires were started among The M/T; on the whole, another good day. No flak was encountered.
Bombing 1430-1509, heights 3,000/9,000 feet. 27.3 tons were dropped, two x 4,000 HCNI, 47 x 500 lbs GPNI and 93 x 250 lb GPNI. 115 packets of nickels were also dropped.

Fifteenth Operation: Bombing Bridge at Mojkovac

December 21st, 1944

Wellington 'J' NA720
W/O GAUNT: pilot

Shadows of the Past

Sgt SCANLON: navigator
Sgt SANDELL: bomb aimer
Sgt McMELLIN: wireless operator
Sgt HAZELDEN: rear gunner
Up 1337 hrs, down 1632 hrs.

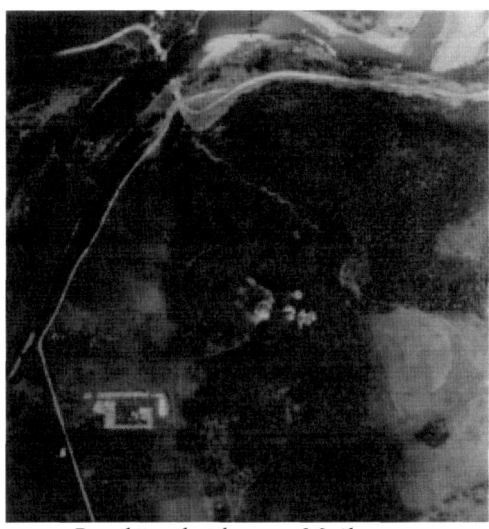

*Bombing bridges at Mojkovac.
Photo: Alan Isaac.*

Details of Sortie
Foggia Tortorella – Mojkovac Bridge – Foggia Tortorella.

Bridge seen and bomb dropped from 9,500 feet aimed at the bridge (one x 4,000 lb HCNI). Bomb undershot about 200 yds.

December 23rd: no operations by group owing to adverse weather.

December 24th: no operations by group owing to adverse weather.

Summary of Events
Seven aircraft took off to destroy Mojkovac Bridge. The weather was good and all a/c clearly saw the target. No hits were claimed, but two of the attacking aircraft reported seeing the bridge destroyed. One crew said they saw what was a 4,000 pounder demolish the target. The destruction is confirmed by photos, but it is not known whether it was caused by an a/c of this or another squadron. Bombing 1507-1526 hrs. Heights 5,500-9,000 feet. 18.75 tons were dropped, comprising two x 4000 lb HCNI, 34 x 500 lb GPTI and 26 x 250 lb GPNI.

Shadows of the Past
  Sixteenth Operation: Bombing Railway Bridge at Casarsa

December 26th, 1944

Wellington 'H' MF367
W/O GAUNT: pilot
Sgt SCANLON: navigator
Sgt SANDELL: bomb aimer
Sgt McMELLIN: wireless operator
Sgt HAZELDEN: rear gunner
Up 1609 hrs, down 1940 hrs.

Details of Sortie
Foggia Tortorella Casarsa railroad bridge Foggia Tortorella.

Target was clear but hazy. Red TI seen. Bombs dropped in one stick nine x 500 lb GPTI and four x 250 lb GPTI from 7,000 feet aimed at red TIs to hit west end of bridge. Burst seen to straddle west end of bridge.

Summary of Events
Casarsa Railway Bridge.

Casarsa railway bridge over the Tagliammento River is of vital importance to the Germans in North Italy at a time when every effort is being made to thoroughly disrupt communications. The group therefore was given a change from Yugoslavia and 15 a/c from our Squadron went out with Liberators, other Wellingtons and target marking aircraft of 614 Squadron, the target was well illuminated and marked.

Only slight inaccurate HFF and LFF was encountered. A good concentration of bombing was achieved. However, photos taken by our aircraft do not suggest that the target was hit, though several crews claim to have straddled it and one or two crews believe they obtained hits on the west end of the bridge. Weather good in target area, little haze. Bombing 1230-1735 hrs. Height 6/9,000 feet. 38.5 tons were dropped, comprising 2 x 4,000 lb HCNI, 112 x 500 lb GPTI and 52 x 250 lb GPTI.

Seventeenth Operation: Bombing Casarsa Bridges

December 28th, 1944

Wellington 'F' MF243
W/O GAUNT: pilot
Sgt SCANLON: navigator
Sgt SANDELL: bomb aimer
Sgt McMELLIN: wireless operator
Sgt HAZELDEN: rear gunner
Up 1604 hrs, down 2011 hrs.

Details of Sortie
Foggia Tortorella Casarsa railroad bridge. Both bridges seen, also flares and reds. Five bombs dropped in one stick from 6,800 feet aimed at red target indicators. Stick believed to have straddled bridge.

Summary of Events
Casarsa Railway Bridge. It appears that Casarsa railway bridge is still standing, it is again the target for the Group. 12 a/c took off from the Squadron, the weather was good. The illumination and target marking by 614 Squadron was excellent. A good concentration of bombing was achieved, but results were largely unobserved owing to smoke and glare from markers. Moderate inaccurate H/FF was encountered.

Photo Received. Reports received since both attacks now indicate that the bridge suffered considerable damage on 26th. The western approach was damaged, there was a direct hit on the centre rendering it impassable and the diversion over the river was also damaged. Later, the 14th span from the west collapsed, further damage was caused on the second raid.

Shadows of the Past

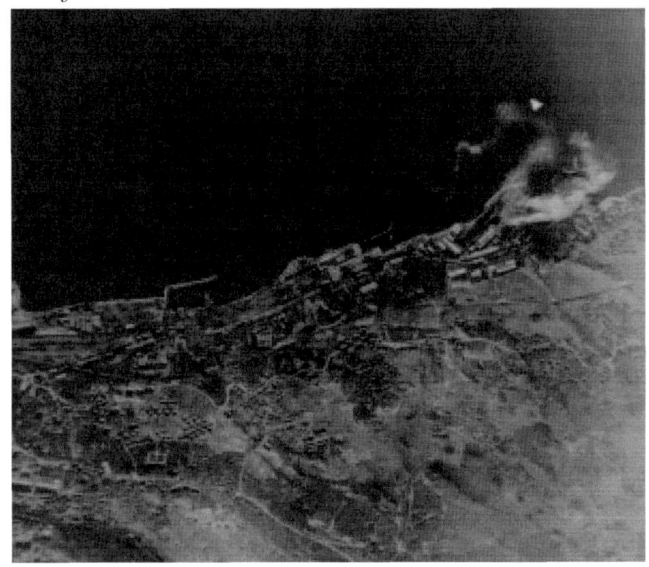

Bombing Fiume (Rieka), February 16th, 1945. Note the Wellington at low level, top right.

Triest Harbour, 1945: all ships sunk or damaged.

Shadows of the Past 165

Bombing Rogatich, November 23rd, 1944.

Bombs away: Roghtich, Jugoslavia, November 1944.

Chapter Seven

Eighteenth Operation: Supply Dropping, Udine

January 8th, 1945

Wellington 'G' LP614
W/O GAUNT: pilot
Sgt SCANLON: navigator
Sgt SANDELL: bomb aimer
Sgt McMELLIN: wireless operator
Sgt HAZELDEN: rear gunner
Up 1125 hrs, down ?

Details of Sortie
Foggia Tortorella – nothing heard from the aircraft after taking off from base – a later message states that the crew are safe and in Partisan hands. January 6th – 7th, Group did not operate owing to adverse weather.

Summary of Events
Nine a/c took off to drop supplies to Partisans near Civcaino in NE Italy, Udine area. There was 10/10 cloud over N/Italy which prevented observation of the ground signal. Eight a/c brought their containers back to base. The ninth a/c, Warrant Officer Gaunt PH (captain) and crew did not return to base and no message was received. It has since become known that the whole crew is in partisan hands and further details are awaited.

Tubby Gaunt's Crash Landing
January 7th - February 8th, 1945
Vode-Gerovo-Zada

January 8th, 1945
The weather conditions were very severe, the previous two days Group did not operate owing to the adverse weather conditions. At briefing, the Wellington crews learned that the day's operations were to drop supplies to the partisans in the Circhino area in north east Italy. Nine

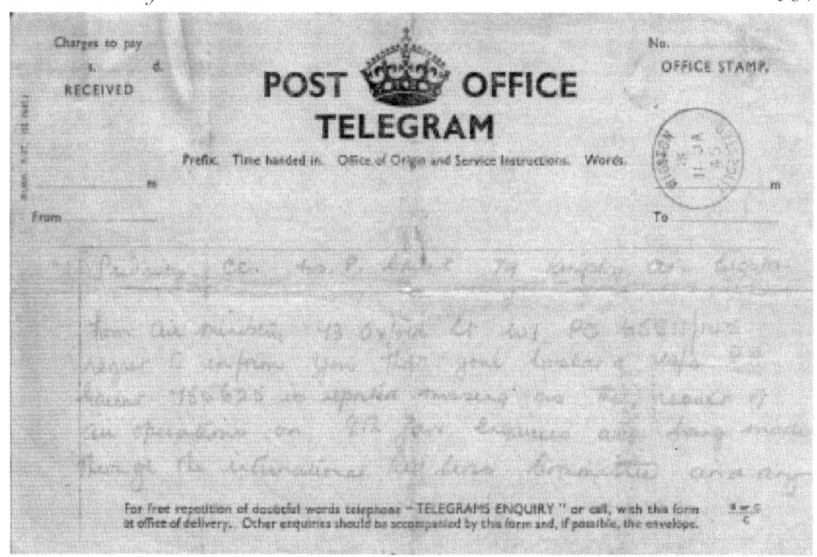

Telegrams received by Florence Gaunt, Tubby's wife.

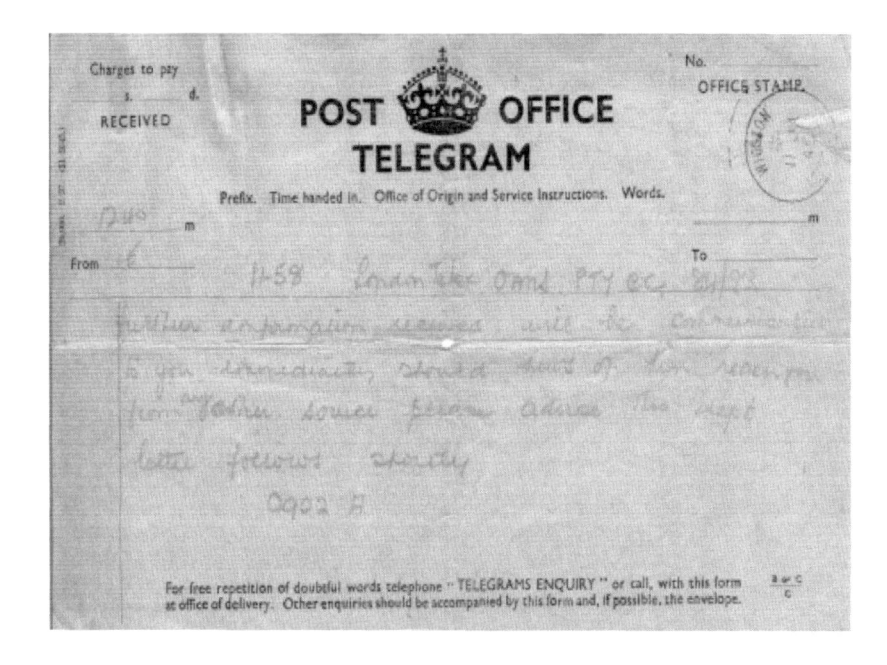

Shadows of the Past

Tubby's Wellington crashes in a dramatic flurry of snow.

Shadows of the Past

Shadows of the Past

aircraft were to take part from 'A' & 'B' Flight of 70 Squadron, the following operated: 'A' Flight Sergeant Collins, 'C' Pilot Officer Jaiiques, 'G' Warrant Officer Gaunt. 'V' Flying Officer Hargreaves, 'P' Flight Lieutenant Pearce, 'S' Sergeant Old, Flight Sergeant Humphries, 'X' Sergeant Mosely, and 'O' Pilot Officer Cox.

(Scats) Maurice Sandell, Tubby's bomb aimer recalls: -

'Take off time was 1125 hours, we flew straight out over the Adriatic and set course north for Italy, conditions were far from good and we were soon flying totally blind. At the briefing we were informed that the ceiling height would be 16,000 feet and the safe flying height over the mountains was 10,000 feet. On reaching the dropping area, neither the ground or the ground signal was seen due to 10/10 cloud all over the North East Italy area. There was deep snow throughout the North Italian area and Yugoslavia, making dropping signals to be easily seen from the air when visibility was good. In daylight drops it was usual to either dig a large cross out of the snow or mark the surface with pieces of material. When there were continual falls of snow, the dropping area would be cleared daily, some areas were safer than others and could be used safely many times, until the Partisans moved them due to enemy activity. Tubby decided to abort the drop and return the containers (six of them) to Foggia. Soon afterwards we flew into a large area of storm clouds, we were being thrown about and the wings looked as if they would flap off. The instruments went completely crazy, the aircraft was being thrown on its nose. Each time any loose kit and the endless amounts of mud that had been brought into the aircraft on our boots splattered all over the instrument panel and the crew'.

Conditions continued to become worse, the fuselage and wings were icing up, loud clattering noises were to be heard as the ice forming on the propellers flew against the side screen and fuselage. Tubby was concerned now, the aircraft was gradually losing height, the build up of ice was at danger-levels and becoming worse every minute.

Suddenly, they broke cloud and Scats explained they were approaching the sea, the white caps they thought was the sea, were in fact the snow covered fir trees clinging to the mountain sides, they were over Yugoslavia,

(Copy)   79, Kingston Avenue
          Dyson Field
          Leicestershire
          England
          7-2-45.

The Commanding Officer
   N° 70 Squadron
      C.M.F.

Dear Sir,
       I am writing to you on behalf of the wife of N° 755625, Warrant Officer, Philip Henry Gaunt, missing from operations, January 8th, 1945, while serving under your command, she is very anxious to become acquainted with the relatives of the other members of his crew, with the hope that some information, other than that from official sources, may be forthcoming.
       It would also be gratifying if you could give any details, as to the mission, whether any visible evidence was reported, from other crews on the same operation.
       Trusting you can furnish us information, which news may have come to your notice, as will allow, small, and appease our anxiety.

Letter written by Maurice on behalf of Mrs Gaunt, asking for any further information regarding her 'missing' husband.

Shadows of the Past

70 miles off course. Tubby, pushing the controls forward for more power, it did nothing to regain height, they were now well below the 10,000 feet for clearing the mountains. A quick decision to crash land was made and the crew brought to crash positions. Immediately to the front was a small valley approximately 1,500 yards long, visibility was reasonably good, pushing the stick forward gradually losing height they flew up the valley losing height all the while, a tree broke off the starboard wing beyond the starboard engine. At a few feet above the ground the aircraft took out a line of bushes, finally coming to rest deep in the snow. The impact had ripped open the bomb bay and scooped up snow into the aircraft knee-deep. This was as perfect a crash landing you could get in the conditions.

After a few brief seconds to collect their thoughts, Scats was surprised that no fires had started, this was unusual, most Wellington crashes resulted in appalling fires, making escape or rescue impossible. Coming round after being temporarily stunned, I was aware the aircraft was full of snow. I was sitting on the little flap seat next to Tubby, who was not strapped in, he was bent forward, his forehead was denting the windscreen, he too quickly recovered from the initial impact, Scats opened the escape hatch and said, "After you Tubs". There was a continual drip dripping of fuel from the ruptured wing fuel tanks, speed was paramount to ensure a safe escape. Calling to the rest of the crew, all were free except Geordie Hazelden, he had his legs trapped under the serve feed in his turret. After a brief struggle, Tubs and Scats managed to free him and move off into the waist-high snow, no-one was injured other than small cuts and bruises and being very thankful for it.

Partisans
While the Wellington was crash-landing, a section of friendly Partisans witnessed it all and were soon on hand to help if required, the armed men and women in their green uniforms with red stars on their forage caps, swarmed over the aircraft against the advice from Tubby about the impending fire hazard, they stripped the machine-guns and ammunition out of the turrets, dug down in the snow and wreckage to find the containers and took all the loose equipment they could find. The women began collecting the dripping fuel in small tins, coming from the ruptured tanks.

Partisan HQ at Scrad.

Franja Turk, the English-speaking villager who helped Allied evaders.

We were indeed fortunate to land where we did, not too far away the area was held by the Chetniks and they did not take many prisoners.

Extract From Scats Sandell's Diary

Jan 8*th* 1945 - NEAR GEROVO, YUOGOSLAVIA

After the crash we stayed one night in a house not 50 metres from the stricken Wellington, in the small hamlet called Vode (which means waters). The next day the Partisans took us to the nearest village, Gerovo, this was approximately six km from the crash site. When we arrived, we were introduced to a friendly English speaking fellow, who found us somewhere comfortable to sleep after our journey. We were well fed and warm, little did we realise that this was possibly the last good meal we would eat for five weeks. After a brief chat about our position and possible escape, we settled down for the night. Next morning we were informed that the Partisans were going to organise a courier who would take us by road and across country some 200 miles to Zadar, along no set escape route, by day or night, depending on the enemy activities. Zadar was situated on the coast, the allies were operating a recovery system for

Shadows of the Past

crashed aircrews such as us. A warship would stand off the coast and at a predetermined time, would look for signals from the shore and when a signal was seen would send a small dingy or service boat to pick up personnel. This friendly English speaking man, Franja Turk, would be our courier from Gerovo to Brod Na Kupi.

Jan 10th
A stay of two days in Gerovo and much rested, the party headed out on the road to Skrad, walking and resting, the journey along the snow covered roads was not easy. How glad we were of our warm flying kit, our boots were ideal for the frozen ground. Climbing and descending the mountain roads for about 12 miles, we eventually reached a small town called Brod in the early evening. Tubs and I were bunked together, the weather was now extremely cold, we were fed on a variety of nuts and a local plonk called 'Riaguia'. Our stay was to be for one night only. We were joined by our couriers, Miro and Vodnik, who were to take us through to Zadar.

Jan 11th
We left Brod early morning, our guides Miro/Vodnik informed us we were on our way, hopefully we would reach Skrad where the Partisan Headquarters were. We said goodbye to our friend Franja and thanked him for his help and hospitality. The day's journey took us across some quite high mountains, along tracks, paths and open areas, our guides Miro and Vodnik knew the route well. We arrived late in the afternoon at Partisan Headquarters in Skrad, where we met Captain Harrison, who was the officer in charge of the mission. We were shown our sleeping quarters and given a reasonable but sparse meal. After we were offered some real cigarettes, making ourselves as comfortable as possible, we were to be here for six days. We had settled in well by the time we had to move on. Before we left for the next part of the journey, we were joined by two Dutchmen, who were to be with us for the next couple of weeks.

Jan 17th
Captain Harrison sees us off and wishes us well.
We are on our way again, very cold today, arrived at Morovitch late afternoon. We had to split up and Tubby and I were shown into a small

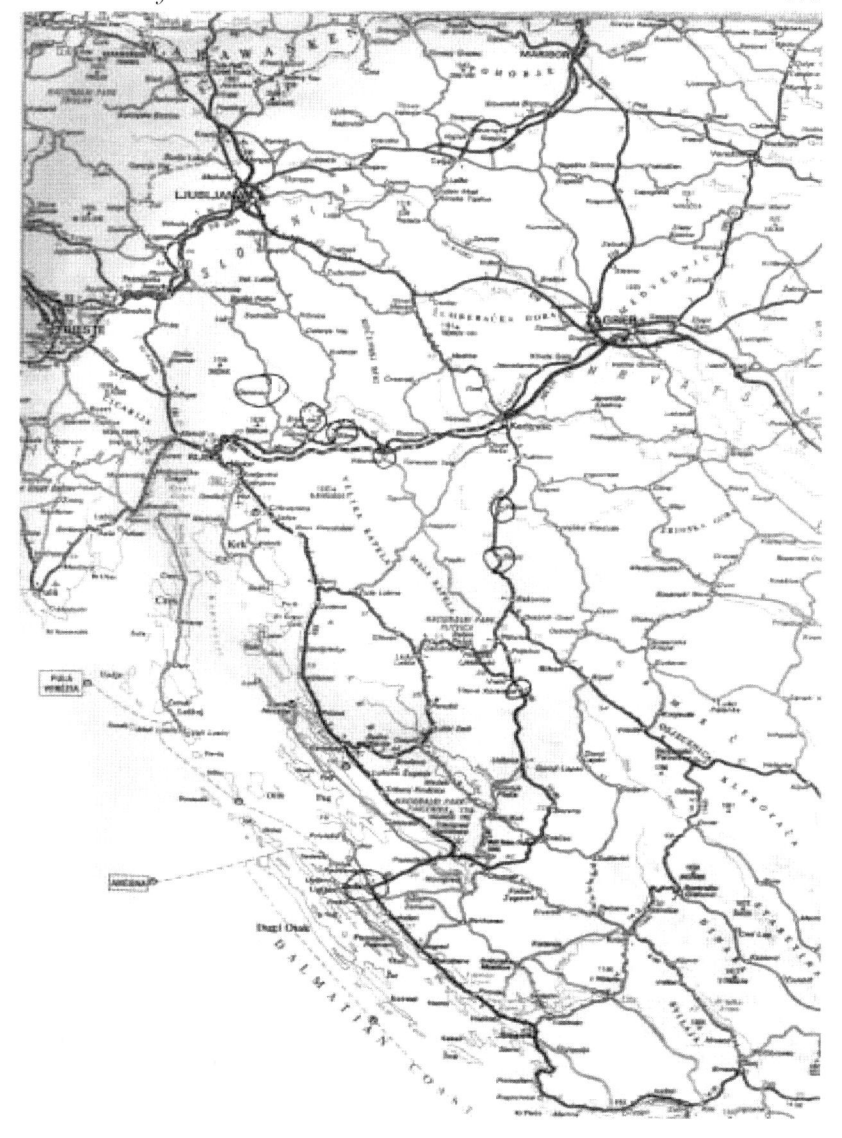

NE Croatia, showing crash site & route of repatriation.

Shadows of the Past

house. The people were very poor, they had little possessions and hardly any food, but they fed us, we were very tired - still hungry and "cheesed-off".

Jan 18th
Continuing our journey, we are heading for a small town called Verbosk. Starting early, approximately 0600 hours, walked quickly all morning, we stopped off with peasants, who fed us as well as they can, time 1300 hours. These people are very good and excellent company. Because of enemy activity, we must stay low until nightfall, leaving as soon as it was dark, we walked until we reached Verbosk. Slept in abandoned building, made our own meal supplied by the peasants we left earlier in the day, our courier, Miro, told us the townsfolk were fascists, we were unimpressed, and soon asleep.

Jan 19th
Started late today, 1330 hours, had a good rest. The cold is extreme, we have been walking some time, Miro informs us we will cross the jerry lines tonight, this makes us more aware, we walk all through the night until 0730 hrs on the 20th Jan. This part of the journey has been the worst yet, felt just like packing in, very tired and weak. Ended journey in boat house on river bank. We have no food and are extremely hungry.

Sleep comes easy, we have just walked some 30 kms over some of the roughest terrain in Yugoslavia, dodging the Germans for over seven hours.

Jan 20th
An early start again, walked through very barren country, our tracks very visible in the snow. Reaching a river, we crossed it, reached the village of Velune, started a very unpleasant stay. Miro informs us that transport in the form of a sleigh should arrive in the morning, if not, possible wait of three or four days. We have very little food, just bits and pieces of this and that. The children in the village have coughs and scabies and are generally in poor health. The women spit on the floor and the chickens sleep on the beds. We were made very welcome, but they had little to offer. We almost prayed daily for transport to take us away. Good news today, sleighs on the way.
Jan 24th

Shadows of the Past 177

At last the sleighs are here, we say our goodbyes and move off quickly along the mountain roads towards the town of Slunj. Arriving late afternoon, we all sleep in a very cold derelict building with a group of Partisans. We discover that there are some Americans in the town. We all move over to where they are, much warmer and a little more comfortable, also some food. The next morning, we say farewell to our couriers, Miro and Vodnik, who had brought us through safely from Skrad, some eighty miles or so over the roughest most inhospitable country we had ever seen. The two Dutchmen leave us and continue to another destination. Our stay here seems forever, we are getting bored and after a few days we look forward to Thursday, Market day, everything happens on market day. The little food available is on sale, and everything else, from an axe to a cupboard. We are here for nearly two weeks, awaiting a convoy of lorries to come from Zada, bringing arms ammunition,

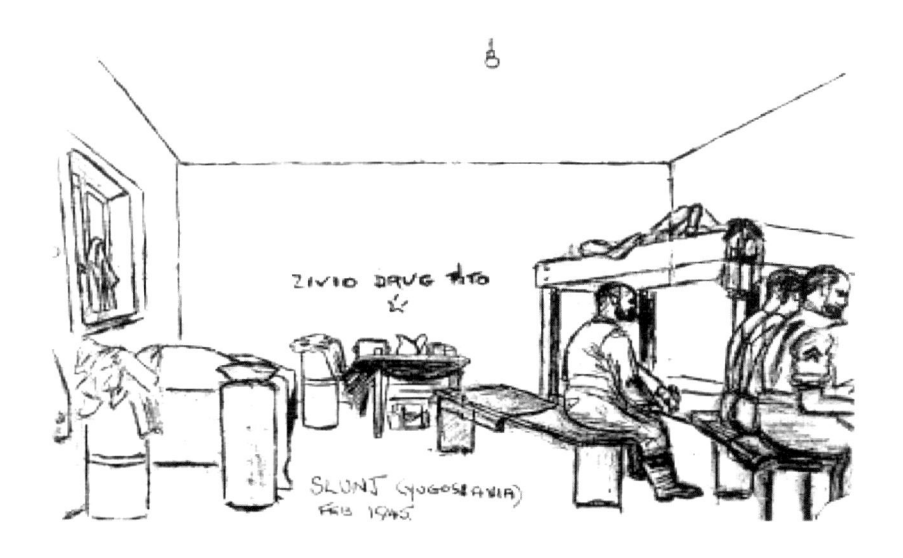

A sketch by Geordie Hazelden of conditions at Slunj, February 1945. Tubby is sitting below the bunk where Americans play cards, Scats Sandell lies on the top bunk.

Shadows of the Past

medical and food supplies for the Partisans, to then return hopefully with us?

Feb 5th
At last we leave Slunj in the convoy, a dozen or so lorries altogether, the snow has lessened and the roads are a little better. The convoy gathers speed and we cover a good few miles, the further we travel the better the roads become. We make the wreckage of Korenice by nightfall, a distance of some 40 miles, we were met by a damn good major, who showed us to a small shack that was under probable shelling seven kms away. Awoke next morning and told we move on today, "good show".

Feb 6th
Said our goodbyes to Korenice, our next destination Zadar, we travelled carefully along wicked roads to the coast, a distance of some 80 miles or so. We travelled all day from 0600 hours until 1600 hours and stopped to refuel and have a bite to eat. After 30 minutes we are on our way again, hopefully straight through to Zadar. The weather does not look good, plenty of snow in the clouds, but it stays fine, no snow and the roads are quite clear of snow as well. We have a good climb over the mountains and descend from 6,000 feet, really glad when we reached sea level. Reached Zadar at 2115 hours, taken immediately to service boat and taken out to British Cruiser, our first real meal for weeks, and many cups of good navy char. Slept on good camp beds and very comfortable they were too.

Feb 7th
Our last day in Yugoslavia, awoke to more cups of tea and a good English breakfast, a proper wash and tooth clean, "how wonderful". We said our thanks and farewells, left cruiser and transferred to destroyer, at last we felt safe and on route to Bari, Southern Italy.

The journey had taken five weeks, we all lost some two - three stone in weight and I made a personal pledge then that after the war I would never go without food again. On their return to England all five crew wore their coveted flying boot badge with justified pride.

Shadows of the Past
Notes from Joseph Kilobucar
(Croatian Aviation Enthusiast)

KUPJAK GORSKI KOTAR CROATIA

It is not remembered by Scats if he thought that the guards accompanying them were just guards or couriers as well. Talking to the other crew members, a Partisan nurse went with them all the way through to Zadar. She was dressed in Partisan uniform and had much in the way of personal weapons, hand grenades, pistol, submachine gun and ammunition and a small amount of ammunition among a sparse first aid kit, with various wound dressings. As already stated, Franja Turk was their courier from Gerovo to Brod-Na-Kupi. The next Partisan courier was Matija Glad, he was very knowledgeable about the mountainous area, between Brod-Na-Kupi and Skrad.

Matija Glad was born on December 24th, 1896 and died, aged 85, on April 2nd, 1981. He was Partisan Guide for six airmen (Gaunt's crew of five plus one other) in January 1945.

The route on this part of the escape for the walking group was Brod Na Kupi, Zamost, Pavka, Golik, Dolnje, Raskrizje, Gornje, Raskrizje, Gorica, Planina to Skrad. The group stayed in the Partisan headquarters in the villa (Verin Bor). Villa Verin Bor (Vera's Pine) was the most beautiful house in Skrad between WWI and WWII. It was owned by a rich industrialist, who owned a saw mill and a brick factory.

<u>Scats Sandell's Jugoslavian Diary – Written as it Happened.</u>

Jan 8th, 1945
Entered cloud to identify target. Encountered ice and bad conditions. Instruments clogged and lost when eventually broke cloud. Impossible to maintain height and crash-landed in valley approx. 6km from village of GEROVO. Partisans took us and handed us over to English speaking F. Turk (a friendly man who spoke English, his name was Franja Turk). Had good food and good bed.

Shadows of the Past

Jan 10th
Been traveling most of day on road to SKRAD. Arrived in BROD in evening and had good feed. Tubs and I were bunked together and were fed by "Ginger" on nuts and riaguia.

Jan 11th
Arrived in late afternoon at partisan HQ in SKRAD. Met Captain Harrison I/C mission. Shown our new sleeping quarters and given food and some real cigarettes. We were becoming quite used to conditions by the time we left.

Jan 17th
Were on our way again and eventually stayed night at MOROVITCH. Tubby and I were shown into a separate place and were very tired and cheesed off. Poor people.

Jan 18th
Been on march all day and were very glad of good meal and good people at lunchtime. Kept waiting till nightfall and finished up at place called VERBOSK. Our courier MIRO told us that the people were fascists but we made our own scoff and soon went to bed.

Jan 19th
Have been walking some time and have been told we cross the Jerry lines tonight. We did. Total time was from 1330 till 0730 on 20th. Worst experience ever. Felt just like packing in. Finished up in boathouse on riverbank.

Jan 20th
Walked from shack to shack and eventually spent night in unsavoury quarters at PERIOSASIS.

Jan 21st
Walked through very barren country. Crossed river again and started very unpleasant stay at village VELUNE. Children had coughs and Scabies. Women spat on floor and chickens slept on beds. We almost prayed every day for transport to get out.

Shadows of the Past

Jan 24th
At last got sleighs and arrived in SLUNJ. Slept first night with partisans in very cold room. Discovered Americans living in town and crept out to sleep in same building. Next morning we said goodbyes to Miro and Vodnik and the two 'Dutchmen" who had been with us since Skrad. The day after we moved in with the Yanks. Everyone sits and waits for Thursday, Market Day. Something to do.

Feb 5th
At last we leave SLUNJ in a convoy that has come in from the coast. The snow seems to have lessened. The road was pretty good and we made the wreckage of KORENICE at night. Met a damn good Major and slept in a shack that was crowded and under a suspense of probable German shelling 7 kms away. Awoke next morning and told we move today. Good show.

Feb 6th
Said goodbye to Korenice and kept going over wicked roads to coast. Arrived at 16.00 hours at a place for a meal and told we go through tonight. Snow clouds overcast and a climb over the coastal mountains. Made a descent of about 6,000 feet. Really glad when we made sea level. Arrived at ZARA at 9.15 (21.15 hours) and put aboard a cruiser.

Feb 7th
Had good night on cruiser. Drank some good Navy char and smoked some real cigs. Slept on camp bed and greeted the morn with a good wash down and tooth clean. Left cruiser at 1007 and went aboard a Destroyer. At last on move to Italy.

Chapter Eight

Looking for Information in Slovenia & Croatia

During my research into this story, there have been, from time to time, instances when one has wondered if some things are meant, or is it pure luck or quantified judgement. Having found Gerovo as the nearest village to the crash site in Yugoslavia, I decided one Friday afternoon that I would enquire at the local travel agents about possible flights to either Zagreb, Croatia, or Ljubljana, Slovenia. As I wanted to fly immediately, security would allow only the Zagreb flight on the Sunday, two days later.

With prior information of the whereabouts of the Modern History Museum in Ljubljana, which I thought would be able to throw a little light on my enquiries, ready for a holiday with my partner, I booked the flight to Zagreb.

Arriving in Zagreb, we took a taxi to the city centre where we booked into a hotel. After settling in, we walked down to the railway station and bought two tickets to Ljubljana. Our train left at 8.30 a.m. on Monday. The journey took two hours through some of the most beautiful countryside I have ever seen. The railway followed the river Sava that wound its way through the hills covered with fir and beech trees. Arriving at Ljubljana station, the enquiry office staff were magnificent, finding a hotel just 400 metres from the Museum, which was also close to the city centre.

Arriving and full of excitement, I walked down to the Museum, knocked on the doors, only to find that the museum is closed on a Monday. My disappointment was lifted when the doorman assured me the museum would open at 10 a.m. on Tuesday. My partner, Denise, and I then set off to see the city. The brochures were not wrong, what a truly lovely city Ljubljana is. Easily covered in a day if you want a quick look around, but really three to four days to see everything properly. The architecture is wonderful and the bars and restaurants have to be tried and seen.

Shadows of the Past

Tuesday arrived and reaching the Museum, we went in and started to follow the organised route around the exhibition. On reaching a seated area, the room was totally surrounded with enlarged photos of the Partisan campaign during the second world war, a sound track was played and various gun fire at irregular intervals enhanced still pictures being flashed across all the four walls. The pictures covered the Partisans struggle during 1941-45. This show made me feel deeply moved.

A young lady, who introduced herself as Josephine, spoke to us. I commented on the very poignant exhibition and continued to tell her why I had come to Ljubljana. Josephine beckoned us out of the exhibition and along a corridor to a lovely little study where she introduced us to another polite young lady, whose name is Monica. Explaining our presence, with a wish to obtain possible information about my father's crash and subsequent repatriation, Monica became very excited and enthusiastic, explaining that her colleague, Matthew, was perhaps the country's highest authority on the repatriation of allied airmen during the 1939-45 war in Yugoslavia (Croatia Slovenia as it is now). Monica quickly phoned Matthew, asking him to come immediately to the Museum. He arrived ten minutes later. After we were introduced, he quickly got down to business to find out all he could about my father. We all had a cup of coffee and biscuits. Later, after a couple of hours, Matthew fetched a folder of photos and letters he had accumulated over a number of years. These were of allied aircraft that had come to grief, almost all of them were total wrecks, either blown up in the air or completely wrecked on ground contact. One photo attracted my attention, then another, both were of the same aircraft that was virtually intact. I could not believe my eyes when I saw it was a Wellington bomber. The photo must have been taken some time after the aircraft had crashed because it was covered in fresh snow. I had prior knowledge that the starboard wing of my father's aircraft had been broken off just outboard of the engine, this aircraft was identical. Discovering this photograph gave me a tremendous 'gut' feeling, this was the aircraft I was looking for. The photograph had a date on the back, January 16th, 1945. No other information was available. Monica announced that she knew who the photographer was who took the pictures and that he lived in Ljubljana. His name is Edi Selhaus and he was one of the official reporters and

Shadows of the Past 184

The Museum of Contemporary History, Ljubljana, Slovenia, 1996.

Researching inside the Museum; from left: Monika Mathew, Josephine, Edi & the author, 1996.

Monica, who made everything possible, on our first visit to Slovenia & Croatia, 1996.

Shadows of the Past 185

photographers for the Partisans during the Second World War - what a stroke of luck!

Monica phoned Edi and arranged for him to come and meet us the next day, Wednesday at 10 a.m at the Museum. We all continued to discuss the project well into the afternoon.

Wednesday morning came along soon enough, walking from the hotel to the Museum. As we were approaching the Museum doors, there was an old man just in front of us. I passed a comment that he was the man we were coming to see and sure enough it was. On entering the Museum, we were met by Monica and quickly introduced to Edi Selhouse, a man in his late seventies. Edi and all of us quickly became totally engrossed in our project.

Edi asked for a photograph album from the museum archives, which was found and brought to us in the main office. It was placed on the table. Edi opened it. On the first page, the top three photographs were of a crashed Wellington Bomber. On turning the page the details of the photographs were printed on the rear. The crash date was January 8th, 1945, at Gerovo. This was indeed my father's aircraft. Edi proceeded to tell us how he took the pictures on or about January 14th. He was directed by the partisans to report and take photographs of the Partisans school at Babno Polji, while photographing the children, they were excitedly telling Edi about their very own aircraft that had recently crashed up the valley a couple of kilometres away. After finishing his assignment, he asked the partisans if he could be taken to the crashed aircraft. Three guards took him and there he took the three photographs we have today. (Since taking the three photos in 1945, Edi new nothing about its crew or circumstances.)

That was all the confirmation I wanted. The next enquiry would take us to Gerovo, a small village 80 miles south west of Ljubljana on the Croatia Slovenia border in the beautiful Gorksi Kotar area. Monica tried to persuade us not to go until the spring because of the deep snow and icy conditions, but I was having none of that. The snow in the mountains at that time was just above half a metre deep, hard work if walking any

Shadows of the Past 186

Top, above & right: Wellington down; three unique snapshots of Tubby's crashed Wellington, taken on January 14th, 1945, by Edi Selhaus.

Shadows of the Past

Shadows of the Past

distance. However, Monica's main concern was the road conditions. Croatia is a poor country and snow clearance is not a priority in the mountain regions. However, arranging a car with good tyres for the trip and contacting one of the veteran Partisans who would in turn contact someone who was aware of the crash site, Vinko Janez who was a retired forester, we said our goodbyes until the next day.

Thursday morning, we were collected by Monica and Matthew at our hotel. Driving south leaving Ljubljana, Slovenia, behind us, we soon reached the border crossing and we see immediately that Croatia is a poorer country. The road immediately continuing over the border was in a very poor state, covered completely with thick ice. The road was bordered on either side by high banks of partly moved snow, in places five feet high. Driving at a reduced speed, we continued very carefully towards Gerovo. The veteran partisan we had to meet was waiting for us outside his home in the village of Caber, just north of Gerovo. He beckoned us in and introduced us to his wife and son. Drinks were offered and we drank more than enough! By midday we felt a lot happier than when we arrived. We moved off to see Vinko, the forester, who as a child of six years old along with his father, had fifty years ago witnessed the crash of Tubby Gaunt's Wellington Bomber. Driving down into the valley, we were in awe of the serenity and beauty of this area, Gorski Kotar, part of the Risniak National Park. Gerovo village nestled in the valley, bringing to mind the perfect Christmas setting.

Arriving in Gerovo, we were immediately made aware again of the very friendly Croatian people who directed us to our contact, the forester, with great enthusiasm. As we approached the comfortable home of the forester, he met us outside in the lane. After the introductions, we all went inside and sat down in the warm snug living room around a larger corner table. Soon we were totally engrossed in our investigations. Vinko was six years old when the aircraft crashed. He recalls seeing the Wellington circle once. He ran through the village to the outskirts to get a better look at the impending crash. There is a large flat area of marshland, which he assumed was to be the landing site. Unfortunately, due to the very short time span involved between breaking cloud and losing height rapidly, Tubby's aircraft actually hit the ground with only

Shadows of the Past

50 metres of clear ground left and sliding along towards a hedgerow with large willow trees spaced along it. The Wellington's starboard wing was ripped off just outboard of the engine by one of these willow trees. This impact, along with the marshy land, stopped the aircraft within a further 80 metres. Either side of the crashed Wellington the land rises, to the left steeply about 200 feet and to the right a 20 feet bank. There were houses that were partially occupied only 50 yards away, the Italians having burnt most of them to the ground. Luck, skill, call it what you may, everyone was in reasonable shape leaving the aircraft as quickly as possible in case of impending fire. That didn't happen, thankfully. The actual crash site was in Vode, a small hamlet 5/6 km from Gerovo.

Just arrived: Gerovo, 1996, Mathew, Denise & I.

The forester, Vinko, was vague about other crash recollections. Talking further about the impact of the crash on the local villagers, he went on to say the containers carried by the bomber had uniforms and ammunition inside. The Partisans took all the latter and also every loose item in the aircraft, guns, ammunition, radio, Very pistol, just everything. The villagers were to be seen dressed quite smartly in the British battle dress uniforms over their white parachute silk shirts. Once the Partisans had removed everything they wanted from the stricken aircraft, it was open to pickings by any one. Vinko's two uncles were in dispute as to who would have the dingy. After a long period of deliberation they decided to cut it in half and have half each. This story brought tears of laughter from our party, who by now were tucking into lavish helpings of sausage, cheese and fresh bread, washed down with glasses of wine and brandy (Rakia).

Shadows of the Past

Bogden Turk, veteran partisan from Cabar.

Bogden & Vinko, outside the latter's house in Gerovo.

Shadows of the Past

The crash site, 1996. From left: the author, his wife, Denise, Vinko Janez, Monica Kokalj Kocevar & Bogden Turk.

The author's late friend, Miljenko (Mile) Malnar points out the exact impact spot,

Tito's Partisan's & the Opposition Party's Fighting Units

Hitler's invasion of Yugoslavia in April 1941 threw the country into ever increasing instability. King Peter was to seek refuge in England.

General Mihailovic and his followers were called the Chetniks formed from the Royalist Army of King Peter II, along with other surviving elite of Jugoslavia. Mihailovic, because of his high ranking followers, was to suffer much in the way of murderous blackmail pursued relentlessly by the Germans, who retaliated against guerrilla activities by shooting batches of between four and five hundred people, mainly civilians, from the Belgrade area.

This had the effect of slowing down and in some areas stopping guerrilla activities altogether. Mihailovic was seen to fraternise with the German and Italian invaders, giving them certain non-aggressive areas throughout the Balkans.

By the autumn of 1941, Serbian guerrilla activities had almost stopped completely.

It was the Communist Party headed by Tito who rallied the common people of Jugoslavia and who would take the battle against the Axis Forces forward.

Tito was to give the ordinary people a cause to fight for they had precious little to lose other than their lives. He was to instil in them a pride and will to overcome the Axis Armies by the familiar hit and run war of the guerrilla army. This band of men were to become known as the Partisans, who were ready to fight to the last man. Death was not a problem. This was something the Germans and Italians had not encountered with Mihailovic, the shooting of hostages that had the desired effect, suddenly was not effective in stopping guerrilla activities. The guerrillas in their mountain hides had to be found, which required much planning and resources, and would ultimately lead to many German and Italian casualties. The guerrilla forces were to grow month by month from a few men and in three years to many divisions by 1945. Reprisals and battle casualties would not deter them from becoming Partisans. For the common man it was either death or freedom.

The internal troubles in the Balkans were to explode. The Partisans would soon be in conflict with the Cetniks who were making bargains for immunity with the Axis Forces. The Serbian Partisans deliberately violated any agreements made with the enemy by the Cetniks, the Germans then shot Cetnik hostages and as a result, the Cetniks would give the Germans information about the Partisans. All this was to happen sporadically and uncontrollably in the wild mountain regions of Serbia. It became a tragedy within a tragedy that was unstoppable.

Allied Missions

While these events unfolded, there was nothing the Allies could do to prevent this state of affairs. Some Allied help, however, in the form of a few supplies, were dropped to the few liaison officers who were with the Cetniks. The British Government had until May 1943 only parachuted missions to the Cetnik bands under Mihailovic, who at that time was the official resistance to the Germans through the Yugoslav Government in Cairo. All British liaison officers with Mihailovic were being recalled on the 25th February 1944. This in effect took many weeks.

A new Directive by the Allies was to see many British officers and NCOs being parachuted with radios to Tito's Partisan bands. In command was Captain Deakin, who was to work closely with Tito for the next two years. The British missions soon found that it was the Partisans who were holding down the Germans and not the Cetniks, as previously assumed.

June 1943 was crucial for the Partisans, Tito was fully recognised and the Allies would give all possible support, guns, food and medical supplies, and strengthen the British missions with Tito. A senior officer, Brigadier Fitzroy MacLean, would take control and establish a much larger mission force throughout The Balkans.

Shadows of the Past

MacLean's mission was parachuted into Yugoslavia in September 1943. They found the Partisan Army was being organised at an alarming rate. The Italian surrender during September gave Tito a much needed supply of arms and ammunition. In all, six Italian Divisions had been disarmed by the Partisan forces. Two entire Divisions went over to the Partisans and fought the Germans. In all, the equipment taken from the Italians armed another 80,000 men.

The Partisan army, now totalling 200,000 men and fighting primarily as Guerrillas, was widespread over Jugoslavia, engaging the Germans, who continued their violent reprisals. Churchill was to send his son, Randolph, who would work closely with MacLean at Tito's Headquarters. (While at Slunj Tubby and crew were to meet Churchill. For a few brief moments, Mac McMellin said he thought Randolph was very loud.)

The British Government were to start equipping Tito with tanks, heavy guns, anti tank guns and equipment. This was supplied by amphibious craft, first working through the many islands of the Dalmation Coast.

Supply Drops to the Partisans

The British missions working throughout the Balkans with the Partisans used their radios to contact other Partisan units and the British Headquarters in North Africa and later Brindisi and Bari in Italy. The long lists of supplies, including food, medicine, uniforms, arms and ammunition, was transmitted through with the coordinates for the dropping zones. At night fires and torches were used, by daylight various ground signals, a cross in the snow was used using black sacking cloth, or an X, if the snow was deep a cross or X would be dug out baring the dark soil.

These special dropping places were sometimes in areas occupied by the Axis and others in Partisan liberated territory. Later, as landing strips were cleared and built, the planes also landed, these were mainly Dakota twin engine transports that brought supplies in and the injured Partisans out, also expectant women, children and allied airmen who were being repatriated.

Shadows of the Past

In the northeast part of Yugoslavia there were 30 dropping places and 3 airstrips, the biggest dropping area was Cerkno in south west Slovenia.

The Partisan movement quickly outstripped the forces of Mihailovic. Croats, Slovenes and large numbers of Serbians along with Italians joined Marshall Tito, who had at this time more than a quarter of a million men at his disposal, along with the large quantities of arms taken from the German and the capitulating Italian Armies.

In Marshall Tito, the Partisans found an outstanding leader, it was perhaps inevitable that these new forces came into battle with General Mihailovic. This internal friction was the cause of many tragic fights and bitter feuds that sprang up between men of the same race and country. The cause that of the common foe.

Domobrani & Ustase

Also in The Balkans were the Domobrani. This fighting unit of about 35,000 men, along with the Ustase, who with the Germans created an independent state, had at their disposal 100,000 men and the White Guards in Slovenia, who came into battle with Tito's Partisans on 9th September 1943 at Turjak. Almost all were killed (around 500 White Guards and Slovenian Chetniks were killed), no prisoners were taken and all the wounded were shot. Those who survived this terrible battle went to Ljubljana and surrendered to the Germans, who organised them into a police force called the Home Guard. The leader of the Home Guard was Leon Rupnik, who was a Slovenian. The main task of this police force was to try to infiltrate and eliminate groups of Tito's Partisans. They also defended villages around Ljubljana from Partisan attack and also prevented loyal peasants to Tito's Partisans from giving them assistance and food.

The Ustase, a fascist organisation, was created in about 1929 by a fanatical Croatian nationalist, Ante Pavelic. It operated violent terrorist action against orthodox Serb establishments of Jugoslavia throughout the 1930s. Pavelic and the Ustase being in control of the nominally Independent State of Croatia after the fall of Jugoslavia in 1941, perpetrated appalling

Shadows of the Past

brutal purges against non-Croat nationalities, Muslims, Orthodox Serbs and Jews, within their control. At the end of the war equally devastating atrocities were committed against Ustase sympathisers in reprisal. During the last weeks of fighting in Europe, the remnants of the Croatian Army, along with Cetnik forces, Ustase and Home Guard, were crushed by the dominant forces under Tito, sympathisers for these anti-Tito forces were pushed north into Austria, numbering approximately 150,000. Along with retreating units of the German Army, this mixed group were returned to Tito shortly after the war and were marched south through Slovenian territory towards Maribor, where a large contingent of Ustase joined the growing group of refugees. After a couple of days this huge group of opposition refugees disappeared. It is only recently that many mass graves have been found.

Slovenian Partisans

The war in Jugoslavia was to become a war within a war until all these other fractions were eliminated. Tito was to become a very powerful and undisputed leader of the whole of Yugoslavia. He was to succeed in winning the sympathy of all the Feruling portion of the patriotic Slovenes, who believed that the main enemy of the nation was the Nazi occupiers and were prepared to fight. The first more or less spontaneous sabotage activities in Slovenia occurred in April 1941, the first clash with the Italians occupying forces took place 13th May 1941. On 22nd June 1941 the Slovene Partisan Army Headquarters was founded. By the end of the year it had 32 units in seven battalions under its command (around 40,000 combatants).

In the spring of 1942, Ljubljana, the centre of Slovenia, where the Partisan resistance radio stations and numerous underground presses with a well organised distribution of resistance news had been operating since 1941, was surrounded by thirty-four kilometres of well guarded barbed wire fence.

The Italian surrender on 8th September 1943, as already said, gave the Partisans much needed arms, also many thousands of prisoners were released by the Partisans and these men joined the Partisans who rescued them or walked home and joined their local Partisan units. The organising

Shadows of the Past

of the British missions throughout Yugoslavia with the Partisans enabled the supply of explosives and arms to carry out the extensive sabotage operations against the main lines of communication in Slovenia, Croatia and Bosnia.

It was mid-1943 that the Allies sent the first mission to Slovenia. It was led by a Canadian, Major William Jones. Soon after he landed, the supplies started to be dropped to the various units of the Slovenian Partisans.

The first frontal battle between Slovenian Partisans and the Wehrmacht was at Drazgose, a village in the German controlled upper Carniolia (Gorenjska region). The battle was to last several days and resounded strongly throughout Europe. The Germans responded sharply with reprisals executing large numbers of hostages, burned down entire villages and sent many people to internment labour and concentration camps (such as Gonars in North Italy 80 kilometres west of Ljubljana). These camps such as Gonars were used primarily by the Italians, the Germans also sent members of the civilian population to Gonars and their own labour and concentration camps such as Dachau, Mauthausen and Ravensbrueck. One of the most brutal acts of intimidation and reprisals occurred in February 1945, ninety-nine hostages were hanged from trees lining the road in Frankolovo after a Nazi official was ambushed and shot dead.

The Germans wanted to fulfil Hitler's order 'Macht mir dieses land wieder Deutsch' and the old phrase, a great Germany from the Baltic to the Adriatic, by sending 63,000 Slovenes, from a cross section of society, into exile to Croatia, Serbia and Germany. They settled German Volksdeutsche from Kocevje in some cleared areas, but faced by early Partisan resistance in the northwest part of Slovenia, had to postpone this plan (Upper Carniolia). Nevertheless, they continued to carry out their intentions through the inhumane policies they were accustomed to practising on other populations, condemned to extermination; exile deportation to concentration camps, imprisonment, killing hostages, stealing children from parents and burning houses and villages.

Sabotage: railway engines derailed by partisans.

American airmen with partisans at Kotjansko (NE area of Slovenia), 1944.
Photo: Museum of Contemporary History, Ljubljana.

Partisans burning railway sleepers, destroying 200 metres of track a time.

Bridge destroyed by a joint British/Partisan mission.

Partisans using radios supplied by the Allies.

All photos Museum of Contemporary History, Ljubljana.

Shadows of the Past

One such atrocity was carried out near the small Serbian town on the eastern side of Yugoslavia called Kragujevac. German troops had clashed with Partisans in that area and a number of Germans had been killed and injured. The Germans in reprisals, it was said, had seized some 7,000 men between the age of sixteen and sixty, arresting them in streets, shops and homes. Being short by three hundred, they took the older boys from schools to make up the required amount.

They proceeded to shoot them in groups of one hundred at a time. Could this be true one asks? Seven thousand when these Germans were not thugs of the Gestapo or the Nazi party, but soldiers commanded by officers (the good guys)? Yet the order for this massacre was produced in due course. The atrocity was then seen to be in pursuance of a Directive issued by Hitler's Chief of Staff, General Keitel, which laid down that in reprisal for the life of one German soldier, the general rule should be capital punishment of one hundred communists, and capital punishment of fifty communists for every injured German soldier. The manner of execution must have a terrorising effect. The total seized for death and injury at Kragulvac, give or take a dozen either way, came out at 7,000. These were driven out for killing to a wooded hillside near the town on 21st October 1941 and there they died along with the 300 schoolboys. The pattern was set, the Hungarian occupiers on the eastern side of Jugoslavia behaved in much the same manner as the German and Italian occupiers. The picture of Jugoslavia in 1941 and through the war had everything nasty about it and leaves nothing to the imagination.

This then gives the reader an insight into the situation that Tubby and his crew found themselves in.

In the north early on in the war, the Italians initially applied a less strict regime. However, they soon followed Mussolini's instructions to make ethnic boarders coincide with Italian state boarders by the end of 1941, with the resistance rapidly growing, the fascist High Commissioner began applying more stringent measures in what was called the Ljubljana Province: he planned mass resettlement of Slovenes, initiated imprisonment, deportations to concentration camps, burning of villages and killing of hostages like his German counterpart. In addition, there were 3,700 military court mock proceedings against 13,000 accused.

Day to Day Life for the Partisans

The day to day life for the Partisans was hard indeed. The winters claimed limbs and lives. After battles, when heads were counted, frostbite was responsible for up to a third of casualties. Tito and his Partisans became totally dedicated to their wounded. The building of hidden hospitals in the mountains saved many lives, Partisan and Allies alike, many aircrew have those hospital locations to thank, after parachuting and stepping out of their crashed aircraft. In all in the northern Croatia and Slovenia area, some 550 aircrew were rescued and returned to their bases in Italy.

The German and Italian invaders searched sometimes for months and years to find these hospitals, many of which they never found. Those that were found were burnt to the ground and all inhabitants shot – patients, nurses doctors and guards.

The camouflage of these hospitals was carried out first by the initial positioning, usually in a very remote wooded area and built into the hillside. The hospitals were built of wood with the natural bark left on to match the surrounding trees. These hospitals varied in size, some could house 50 patients and doctors, nurses and guards.

To reach the hospitals a very elaborate approach was designed, overhead walkways made from timbers suspended by ropes from trees, tunnels into hillside caves with small openings easy to camouflage. Good use was made of mountain rivers and streams. These could easily cover footprints. One approach was concealed by turning over moss covered stones, walking on them, then turning them the right way up.

Obtaining help from civilian population was not always forthcoming. The Germans and Italians, if they even suspected someone of collaboration, would shoot them and their immediate family, while villages were burnt to the ground and the inhabitants rounded up and shot: men, women, children and babes in arms. One such village called Povhum just east of Rieka (Fiume) in north Croatia was completely destroyed and all the inhabitants slaughtered by the Italian Army. (Visitors to Croatia, on leaving Rieka by motorway heading for Zagreb, are reminded of this sickening violence by a huge granite memorial in the centre of a walled area, that was once the village of Povhum. The residents killed are named on many wall plaques, individuals and complete families.)

The obvious effect on the Partisans for these reprisals was to kill all Italian and German soldiers and their sympathisers without mercy.

Partisan & Civil Casualties

The most recent research in Slovenia produced these figures. By May 1945, 95,000, 6% of the population of the approximate 1.5 million Slovenes spread over the four countries, had been killed, 2,100 in battle and 30,000 as a direct result of the occupation (reprisals, concentration labour camps, forced marches, starvation). Also members of the Home Guard forcibly mobilised Slovenians into the German Army and civilians killed by the Partisans account for the remaining casualties.

The Yugoslav nations suffered great losses in the National Liberation struggle. 305,000 men fell. 425,000 were injured. The losses of the civil population were even greater above all because of the reprisals by the occupation forces and the Quislings (Homeguard, Domobrani, Chetnik, etc). That is why the total losses of all Yugoslav nations numbered over 1,700,000 people or 11% of the population. Over 3.5 million people were homeless at the end of the war. The financial and material damage was estimated at 46.9 million dollars at 1938 prices.

Photographs, pages 201/2: Partisans showing respect to fallen Allied airmen. British mission troops, both officers and NCOs, can be seen in several photographs, together with at least one American officer (wearing dark sunglasses)
Photos: Museum of Contemporary History, Ljublanja

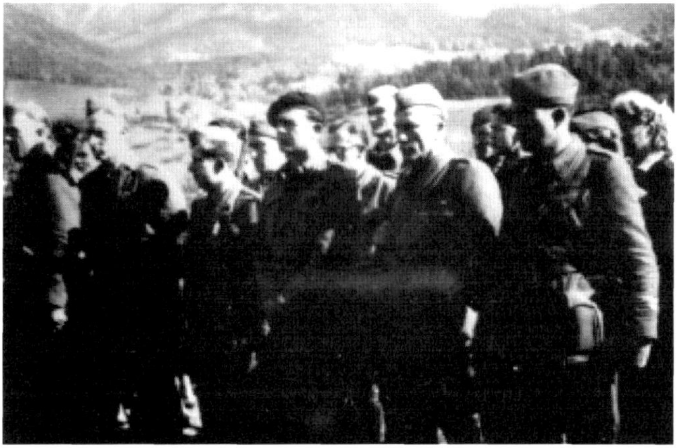

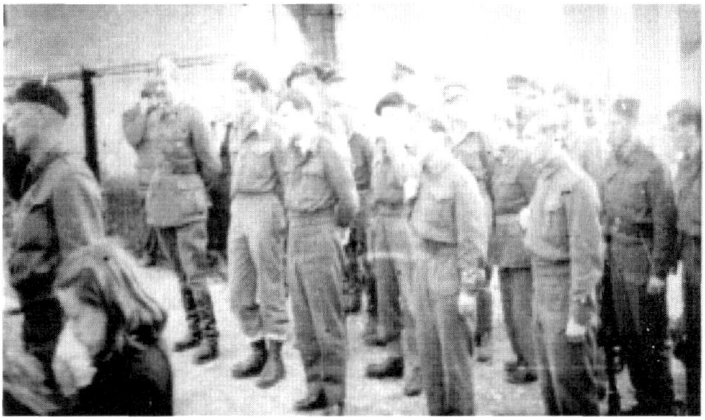

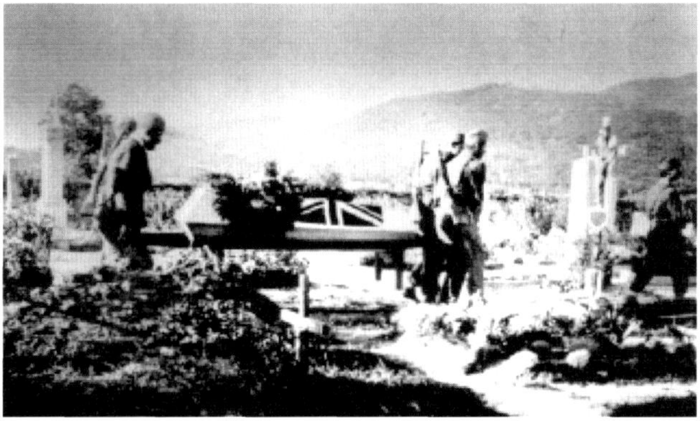

Shadows of the Past 204

Shadows of the Past

A partisan patrol.

A column of partisans moving through deep snow.

Above: Partisans moving in springtime.

Remaining photos 204/5: Partisans of the 43 Istrian Division approaching Cabar (from the direction of Parg Gorski-Kotar).

Shadows of the Past

Postscript

During the early days of my investigations into my father's career in the Royal Air Force Voluntary Reserve, I did not expect to find such a rich and amazing story. Many books I have read about Second World War airmen have been about the specialist, fighter aces and bomber crews who had carried out the more publicised special raids, such as the Dam Busters. Not many aircrew saw out the war. Tubby, however, was one of the lucky ones. His adventures will never cease to amaze me. The enjoyment and pride I have felt while researching his story I will always remember. When people he knew read his story, I know some will be as surprised as me, and for those who did not know him, I hope you will enjoy reading about an airman of the Second World War. This story I hope does not glorify war, it is an attempt to put over to the reader the stress, hardships and constant danger for all aircrew.

November 1945, all three Gaunt brothers safely back from the war; from left: John (aged 16), Arthur, Tubby & Maurice. Peter, the 'Bevin Boy', took the photo.

Tubby Gaunt upon 'demob', 1945.

Dad & Mum, Devon holiday, 1959.

Shadows of the Past 210

Medals, from left: 1939-45 Star, Aircrew Europe Star, Italy Star, 1939-45 Medal, Defence Medal, & Air Efficiency Award.

Insignia: W/O Crowns, A/G & pilot brevets, & the coveted 'Flying Boot'.

Acknowledgements

During the years it has taken me to research and put this story together, I have met and corresponded with many people who have been wonderfully helpful and pleasant. I must apologise for at times, I'm sure, my possibly persistent boring enthusiasm has pushed their patience to the limit! From the start of my investigations, my sincere thanks to Martin Bowman for enabling me to contact Maurice (Scats) Sandell through his book, 'Wellington The Geodetic Giant'. It was Maurice who put me on to Frank (Geordie) Hazelden, Dave (Jock) Scanlon and (Mac) McMellin.

Thanks are also due to the Museum of Contemporary History, Ljubljana, Slovenia, in particular Monica Kokala, Edi Selhaus (whose photographs of partisans can be found at the Museum of Contemporary History), Josephine Sparovec, Mathew Zgajnar. A special thank you to Darinka and Drago Kovac in Gerovo for their friendship, accommodation and help while in Croatia; Partisan veteran Bogden Turk, Vinko Janez, the Forester and his wife Zora, and all the locals in Vode who gave me pieces of the crashed Wellington and the exact position of the aircraft wreck. To the many aircrew and other veterans who gave information about their experiences in the various theatres of war: Peter Merton (IWM Duxford), Norman Mosely (ex-37-70 Sqn, Foggia), Ron Cooper (ex-37 Sqn), Joe Cullum (ex-70 Sqn), Dick Hamer (ex-77 OTU), Geoff Parnell (Air Gunners Association), Bryan Watkins (ex-37 Sqn), L. Thompson (ex-70 Sqn), Bill Hunt (ex-37-70 Sqn), John King (ex-40-37 Sqn), Trevor Stocks (83 Sqn armourer, 1940) and Stan Day, Sgt Pilot, 104 Sqn Foggia Main, who was constantly on tap to answer my questions. Others whose help was equally invaluable were Ken Wright (RAF Desford historian), John Ward & Robin Davis (both 49 Sqn historians), Howard Jones (pilot, 31 & 170 Sqns), the late Doug Skinner (pilot, 104 Sqn), Richard S Robinson (a researcher), the late Bob Foster (air gunner, 70 Sqn), Hew Evans (ex 49 Sqn), Arther F Hornby, Joseph Klobucar (crashed Allied aircraft expert in Gorski Kotar, Croatia), & Juliet at JAM Secretarial Services of Oakham.

Shadows of the Past 212

Thanks are due to my family: my mother, Florence, sister Ann and my other siblings, Christine and Terry, without who's help with the text and photos this work would not be finished.

Thanks also to our friends Tim and Jenny Pratt, who constantly encouraged me to complete the work.

Finally, thanks to my wonderful wife Denise, who has accompanied me on all my quests for information without complaint and given me both understanding and encouragement.

Looking back over the years this project, thanks to so many people, has been so very enjoyable and rewarding.

Thanks everyone!

Bibliography

Wellington: the Geodetic Giant, M. Bowman, Airlife Publishing Limited 1989.
Bomber Crew, J. Sweetman, Little Brown 2004.
Zbogom, Liberty Bell, Edi Selhaus, Janez •erovc, Delavska Enotnost Ljubljana 1988.
Guns for Tito, Major Louis Huot, L. B. Fischer New York 1945.
No 5 Bomber Group, W. J. Lawrence, Faber & Faber Limited.
Wellington Wings, F. R. Chappell, Crecy Books Limited 1992.
Lincolnshire Airfields, Patrick Otter, Countryside Books 2000.
German Capital Ships of World War Two, MJ Whitley, Arms & Armour Press 1989.
VCs of the Air, John Frayn Turner, Airlife Publishing Limited 2001.
The Partisans, David Mountfield, The Hamlyn Publishing Group Limited 1979
Through Darkness to Light, Patrick MacDonald, Images Publishing (Malvern) Limited 1994.
Its Dicey Flying Wimpys Around Italian Skies, Maurice G. Lihou, Air Research Publications 1992.
The Bomber Command War Diaries, Martin Middlebrook and Chris Everitt, Penguin Books Limited 1985.
Beware of the Dog at War, John Ward, Published by John Ward 2004.
The Hampden File, Harry Moyle, Air-Britain (Historians) Limited 1989.
The Second World War, Volume V, Closing The Ring, Winston S. Churchill, The Reprint Society 1952.
Beacons in the Night: With the O.S.S & Tito's Partisans in Wartime Yugoslavia, Franklin Lindsay, Stanford University Press 1993.

APPENDIX

SRUŠENI ZRAKOPLOVI U GORSKOM KOTARU 1942 - 1992
(CRASHED AEROPLANES IN GORSKI KOTAR 1942 – 1992)

Br.	Datum	Zrakoplov	Zemlja	Mjesto pada
01.	25.10.1942	Fieseler Fi 156 Roda	GER	Mjesto nepoznato?
02.	04.11.1942	Caproni Ca 310	ITA	Kupska dolina?
03.	16.12.1942	Heinkel He 111	GER	Treskavac, Lukovo 5 DEAD
04.	10.03.1943	Fiat BR.20 Cicogna	ITA	Josipdol
05.	15.03.1943	Caproni Ca 311	ITA	Vrbovsko-Jasenak
06.	31.07.1943	Caproni Ca 314	ITA	Oštarije-Josipdol
07.	02.11.1943	Dornier Do 17	GER	Mjesto nepoznato?
08.	30.01.1944	Bf 109G-6 Bijeli 2	GER	SE od Udina
09.	23.02.1944	B-24H-10-FO	USA	Samarske Stijene, Mrkopalj
10.	24.02.1944	B-17F-65-BO	USA	Rijeka, Risnjak?
11.	25.02.1944	B-24 #41-29244	USA	Ogulin područje
12.	1/2.03.1944	Bf 109G-6	GER	Liè-Fu•ine. Kobiljak
13.	18.03.1944	B-17G-30-BO	USA	Pogoreli Vrh, Gerovo
14.	18.03.1944	B-17G-25-BO	USA	Bilzu Rijeke
15.	18.03.1944	Bf 109G-6	GER	Guslica, Risnjak (ili 08.04.44)
16.	18.03.1944	B-17G-20-BO	USA	Mlièni Vrh, Platak
17.	18.03.1944	BF 109G-6 Bijeli 4	GER	Blizu Rijeke pilot KIA
18.	18.03.1944	Bf 109G-6 Bijeli 6	GER	Blizu Rijeke pilot MIA
19.	18.03.1944	Bf 109G Bijeli 16	GER	Blizu Rijeke pilot MIA
20.	18.03.1944	Bf 109G-6 Bijeli 18	GER	Blizu Rijeke pilot MIA
21.	18.03.1944	P-47D 42-75742	USA	N od Crikvenice, Veliki Tiæ
22.	18.03.1944	P-47D 42-75736	USA	Dre•nica
23.	19.03.1944	Bf 109G-6 •uti 10	GER	30 km S od Ljubljane ?
24.	28.03.1944	P-38H-5_LO	USA	Crni Lug pilot RTD

Shadows of the Past

25.	02.04.1944	B-17F-40-DI	USA	Lomost, Ogulin
26.	02.04.1944	B-17G-35-BO	USA	Oštarije-Ogulin
27.	02.04.1944	Bf 109G-6 Pik As	GER	N od Crikvenice
28.	02.04.1944	Bf 109G-6 Bijeli 5	GER	Slani Potok, Lukovo pilot POW
29.	02.04.1944	Bf 109G-6 Pik As	GER	Kamenjak pilot POW
30.	2/3.4.1944	Bf 109G-6	GER	Blizu Lièa
31.	06.04.1944	Bf 109G-6 •uti 3	GER	Blizu Ogulina
32.	29.05.1944	Bf 109G-6 •uti 10	GER	50 km S od Zagreba
33.	1944	Bf 109G-6	GER	Viševica
34.	1944	Savez. Lovac s 4 krakom elisom		Jasle Kupjak
35.	1944	Ju 87 Stuka	GER	Vuèja Škulja, Stupaè, Treskavac
36.	07.08.1944	B-24J-190-CO	USA	Blizu Ogulina
37.	20.08.1944	Vickers Wellington	ENG	Mlaèica, Prezid
38.	1944	Bf 109G-6	GER	Turèinovo, Zlobin pilot KIA
39.	06.11.1944	B-24	USA	Iznad Gorskog kotara
40.	06.11.1944	B-24	USA	Iznad Gorskog kotara
41.	15.11.1944	B-24J-50-FO	USA	Blizu Rijeke, Klana
42.	16.12.1944	B-24 #42-52564	USA	Kod Dre•nice
43.	04.01.1945	Halifax V LL 380	ENG	Srebrna Vrata, Risnjak
44.	08.01.1945	Vickers Wellington	ENG	Vode, Gerovo 5 RTD
45.	20.01.1945	B-24J-10-FO	USA	Blizu Rijeke
46.	25.02.1945	Bf 109G-6	GER	Blizu Rijeke
47.	25.02.1945	Bf 109G-6	GER	Jelovka, N od Bakra
48.	20.03.1945	Henschel Hs 126	YUG	Pao u Gorskom kotaru
49.	08.04.19 45	P-51B-15-NA	USA	30 km SE od Rijeke
50.	05.05.1945	Dakota C-47	USA	Lièko Polje, Podkobiljak, Liè
51.	08.10.1948	Jak-3	YUG	Paravièeva Miza, Sne•nik

Shadows of the Past

52.	29.06.1951	Junkers Ju 52/3m	YUG	Risnjak 15 DEAD
53.	01.06.1970	Soko Galeb G2-A	YUG	Mirkovica 2 DEAD
54.	23.06.1978	UTVA-66V	YUG	Gornje Jedi 4 DEAD
55.	21.09.1978	Soko Jastreb J-1	YUG	Ravna Gora – Jasenak pilot KIA
56.	1983	Soko Galeb G2-A	YUG	Gorskom kotaru
57.	29.01.1980	MiG-21	YUG	Prhutova Draga, Èabar
58.	1970	Jedrilica	YUG	Stara Sušica
59.	1980?	Jedrilica	YUG	Kupjak, Leskova Draga
60.	02.1987	Helikopter Mi-2	YUG	Matiè Poljana, Begovo Razdolje
61.	08.11.1991	MiG-21 #26-112	SRB	Medine Drage, Ravna Gora
62.	1945	B-24	USA	Tršæ, Rasadnik

RESEARCH BY JOSEPH KLOBUZER